Copyrighted Material

UExcel-Life Span Developmental Psychology

Gotham City Ventures, LLC
500 Westover Dr. #6479
Sanford, NC 27330

http://www.gothamcityventures.com/

ISBN: 978-0-9964591-0-5

Copyright ©2015 by Gotham City Publishing
All rights reserved. None of the material found in this study guide may be reproduced without permission from the publisher.
Printed in the USA

Disclaimer/Liability Release:
The publication of this book is for the purpose of examination preparation. Gotham City Ventures does not guarantee the accuracy and completeness of the information contained herein and cannot claim liability in relation to the information or opinions contained within this study guide. Gotham city ventures will not be held liable for damages of any kind related to the materials found in this study guide.

Life Span Developmental Psychology

Steps to Achieving Success!

Step 1- Test Taking/Study Skills Review
Gain knowledge in test taking and study skills with over 25 pages of review! Increase your chances of passing the exam by determining your learning style, how to study well and strategies for approaching exam questions.

Step 2- Complete Content Review
Focus on the exam content with a comprehensive review. CreditPrep provides you with a well written and organized presentation of content within this manual and access to online, mobile friendly flashcards. These flashcards allow you to take advantage of every spare moment in your hectic life! Please utilize this valuable resource with the instructions below:

> **FLASHCARD ACCESS:**
> Please go to www.gothamcitypublishing.com
> Click on CreditPrep Flashcards Registration
> Follow the Directions Provided to Access the Flashcards

Step 3- Test Your Knowledge
Use the full length practice exam provided at the end of this manual to determine your knowledge of Developmental Psychology. Use the results of this exam to efficiently focus your final studying efforts.

Step 4- Take Your Exam
Apply the credits earned toward your college degree and future career!!

Life Span Developmental Psychology

Table of Contents

Preparing for Your Exam 8
Study Skills 9
Scheduling Your Test 18
Last Minute Preparation for Testing 18
Test-Taking Tips 19
Multiple Choice Questions 21
True / False Questions 22
Matching Questions 23

Overcoming Test Anxiety 24

Chapter 1: Introduction to Lifespan and Developmental Psychology 27
Overview: 27
Objectives: 27
Developmental Psychology: The Basics: 27
Domains of Development: 28
Development in Context: 29
Approaches to Development: 30
Using an Ecological Approach: 31
Theories of Developmental Psychology: 32
Freud's Theory of Psychosexual Development: 34
Evaluation of Freud's Theories: 36
Erik Erikson's Stages of Psychosocial Development: 36
Classical Conditioning: 38
Operant Conditioning: 40
Reinforcement Schedules: 40
Social Learning Theory: 41
Lev Vygotsky: 42
Information Processing and Memory: 43
Chapter 1: Review 46
Chapter 1 Answers: 49

Chapter 2: Research Methods in Psychology 50
Overview: 50
Objectives: 50

The Scientific Method:	50
Methods:	50
Research Designs:	52
Interpreting Study Results:	53
Ethics in Research:	53
Chapter 2: Review	55
Chapter 2 Answers:	57

Chapter 3: Genetics, Prenatal Development, and Childbirth 58

Overview:	58
Objectives:	58
Concepts of Genetics:	58
Gene-Gene Interaction:	59
Gene-Environment Interactions:	59
Genetic and Chromosomal Abnormalities:	60
Prenatal Development:	61
Childbirth and Bonding:	63
Chapter 3: Review Questions	65
Chapter 3 Answers:	67

Chapter 4: Infancy and Toddlerhood 68

Overview:	68
Objectives:	68
Physical Development:	68
Motor Skill Development:	69
Reflexes:	69
Sensory-Perceptual Development:	70
Nutrition:	71
Cognitive Development:	72
Sensory Coordination:	72
Language Development:	73
Social and Emotional Development:	74
Awareness:	75
Personality	75
Non-Parental Daycare:	77

- Chapter 4: Review Questions 78
- Chapter 4 Answers: 81

Chapter 5: Early Childhood 82
- Overview: 82
- Objectives: 82
- Physical Development: 82
- Cognitive Development: 83
- Language and Grammar: 84
- Social and Emotional Development: 85
- Learning Theories: 85
- Parent-Child Relationships: 86
- Sibling Relationships and Birth Order: 87
- The Media: 88
- Childhood Fears: 88
- Concerns which may arise during Early Childhood: 88
- Chapter 5: Review Questions 91
- Chapter 5 Answers: 94

Chapter 6: Middle Childhood 95
- Overview: 95
- Objectives: 95
- Physical Development: 95
- Cognitive Development: 96
- Language: 96
- Intelligence: 96
- Children with Special Needs: 97
- Social and Emotional Development: 99
- Difficulties of Adjustments: 100
- Possible Conflicts in Middle Childhood: 100
- Chapter 6 Answers: 104

Chapter 7: Adolescence 105
- Overview: 105
- Objectives: 105
- Physical Development: 105

Hormones of Puberty: 106
Health and Hazards of Adolescence: 106
Adolescent Cognition: 107
Adolescent Sexual Activity: 108
Adolescent Morality: 109
Adolescent Psychosocial Development: 109
Parenting and Peers: 110
Vocational Choices: 111
Concerns and Conflicts of Adolescence: 111
Chapter 7: Review Questions 113
Chapter 7 Answers: 116

Chapter 8: Early Adulthood 117
Overview: 117
Objectives: 117
Physical Development and Changes: 117
Concerns and Conflicts of Early Adulthood: 118
Cognitive Development in Early Adulthood: 119
Psychosocial Development in Early Adulthood: 120
Vocational Achievement in Early Adulthood: 124
Chapter 8: Review Questions 125
Chapter 8 Answers: 127

Chapter 9: Middle Adulthood 128
Overview: 128
Objectives: 128
Physical Development in Middle Adulthood: 128
Cognitive Development in Middle Adulthood: 130
Psychosocial Development: 131
Social Dynamics: 132
Chapter 9: Review Questions 134
Chapter 9 Answers: 136

Chapter 10: Late Adulthood 137
Overview: 137
Objectives: 137

Age Related Demographic Changes: 137

Ageism: 137

Physical Changes of Late Adulthood: 137

Health Problems of Late Adulthood: 139

Aging Theories: 139

Cognitive Development: 141

Dementia and Alzheimer's: 141

Psychological Problems: 142

Psychosocial Development Theories: 142

Work and Retirement: 142

Relationships and Intimacy: 143

Conflicts and Concerns of Late Adulthood: 143

Chapter 10: Review Questions 144

Chapter 10 Answers: 147

Chapter 11: Death and Dying 148

Overview: 148

Objectives: 148

Attitudes toward death: 148

The Hospice Movement: 149

The Dying Process 149

Bereavement and Grief: 150

Right to Die and Euthanasia: 150

Chapter 11: Review Questions 151

Chapter 11 Answers: 153

Practice Exam 154

Practice Exam Answer Key 180

Preparing for Your Exam

Chances are if you are reading this, you are a student looking to perform well on an upcoming test. Congratulations, you have taken the first step in achieving that goal. Yes, you have purchased this text, but more importantly this means you have determined to seek success and do what it takes to achieve this success. This means you are already in the right mindset to begin…so why don't we do just that and get started?

Taking a test and performing well is much like a sport. Consider the test to be the "big game" that students face over and over. Every athlete knows the importance of preparing for the game through practice, drills, and training. Just preparing is not enough, the athlete also knows the rules for his or her chosen sport and has developed the ability to remain calm under pressure. Each of these three skills comes together to allow the athlete to perform to the best of their ability and hopefully win the "big game". As a student, you have no doubt heard more than once that tests are designed to demonstrate your knowledge of the subject matter, and while that is true, this is not the entire picture. We have all encountered that student who studies less than everyone yet manages to pass or even get an "A" on the tests they take. Chances are this student not only knows the subject matter, but they know how to play the game. This text is designed to help you understand those "rules" and develop skills that will make you a master test taker. This guide will in no way substitute for knowledge of subject matter, but will certainly assist you in making sure that your test accurately demonstrates that knowledge and that the "rules of the game" operate in your favor. As we move forward, we are going to analyze some study skills that will help you acquire the subject matter knowledge necessary for your test, learn a few test-taking skills that will help you "play the game" even better, and examine how to work well under pressure (relive some of the test anxiety).

Study Skills

Ask almost anyone and they will tell you that the key to success on a test is to know the subject materials for which you are being tested. As we already mentioned, this is only part of the puzzle, but it is an important part. Thus, it is where we will begin our journey together – how to best acquire this subject matter expertise. Our goal here is to help you make the most of the time you invest for studying so that you gain the most knowledge possible in the time you commit to studying.

One of the most important things you can do, as a student, is to determine your learning style. This knowledge will serve you not only for this test, but for every class you ever take. There are a myriad of online quizzes that will help you identify your learning style, but for the sake of brevity we are going to discuss the five basic learning styles here. Chances are you already know how you learn best, even if you have never formally addressed this topic. The five learning styles are described below.

1. Visual learning – has a preference for learning through pictures, graphs, and spatial understanding.
2. Auditory – sometimes called musical – learns best through sound and lectures.
3. Verbal – sometimes called linguistic – process information through words both verbal and written.
4. Kinesthetic – this learner processes by feeling, sensing, and doing
5. Logical – sometimes called mathematical – uses logic and reasoning

If you are a **visual** learner you will want to spend time making graphs, charts, timelines, maps, and pictures that will help you understand the materials. You are going to remember far more about a picture, than information you simply read. If you are an **auditory** learner, then you are one in a small percentage of students who actually do learn through the lecture model that most of western education is built upon. The auditory learner will do best by reading texts books aloud so that they are not simply reading, but hearing the text. Much like the auditory learner, the **verbal** learner should also read test materials aloud. In this case, it is not hearing the content, but in verbalizing it. In addition to spoken word, the verbal learner also learns well by writing information. This makes the practice of note-taking especially beneficial to this learner. The **kinesthetic** learner is often the most challenging for teachers and professors to address. It is the kinesthetic learner who learns best by actually "doing". If you are this type of learner then you need to feel, hold, and manipulate objects in order to best understand the content. This type of learner will learn better while moving around and seldom studies well at a typical desk. Finally, the **logical** learner, needs to understand the "why" behind ideas and concepts. The logical learner needs to see connections and reasons behind the information. Memorization of facts does not typically serve the logical learner as well as a thorough understanding of how the concepts relate to one another. It is important to note here that while one primary sense is usually tied to your learning style, you should incorporate as many senses as possible into your learning routine. So for the visual learner, it is imperative that they see the information in displayed form, but they will also enhance their memory be utilizing their auditory, verbal, and kinesthetic skills. Remember the more senses you can involve in the learning process the better. Don't be afraid to draw, read aloud, sing, or create objects that can be moved in order to see the logic and connections behind the facts.

In addition to the five different learning styles, there are two additional styles that some authors have added. These two are the solitary and social learner. These two types of learners can be found in conjunction with any of the above five learning styles. For example, one could be a solitary visual learner. As the name implies, the solitary learner prefers to learn alone while the social learner prefers learning in the group setting. While the solitary learner is likely to be found alone in the library, the social learner gravitates toward study groups and enjoys group projects that the solitary learner often dreads.

There has been much debate over the years regarding the best time of day to study. The short answer is, there is no one correct answer. The best time of day for study is completely student dependent. If an individual is more alert in the morning then they should study in the morning. If the student is better in the evening, then study in the evening. Most fathers are fond of reminding their children that "you can't hoot with the owls and soar with the eagles." Of course, the preference is typically that you soar with the morning eagles and avoid the night owls as much as possible. However, the main idea serves as a great reminder for students – if you are a morning person make sure to get enough rest to rise early and make use of that time. If you are indeed a night owl, then sleep in and be sure you devote the evening time to study, not just socializing with friends.

With the preliminaries out of the way, let us dive into some more hands on considerations that will help you make the most of your study time.

1. Prepare your space –
    a. Do not study in your bed. Our bodies are conditioned to see the bed as a place of rest and relaxation. By attempting to study in bed, we are constantly fighting the ingrained habit of our bodies. In addition, it can be difficult to fight the constant temptation to take a "quick cat nap" that turns into an hour or two of lost time.
    b. If you do not study in bed, where should you study? Really just about anywhere else that works for you and fits your learning style. Consider a dedicated space that you use only for study. The more you use the space the more your brain will begin to equate the space with productive study.

Life Span Developmental Psychology

    c.   For most students, a desk really is the best option as it not only sets the tone for study and work but also promotes good posture. Many kinesthetic learners benefit from a standing desk or a chair that allows for movement.

    d.   Consider the lighting. Select a space that has good natural light and allows for good artificial light to be added if studying at night. In seeking natural light be cautious of windows. While they do provide great natural light, they can also be a source of distraction. If possible consider this in the placement of your desk. Desks placed to the side of a window allow for good light, but the temptation to gaze into the outdoors is limited by not being situated directly in front of you.

    e.   Gather all your materials. Make sure you study space is adequately stocked with all the necessary materials: books, pens and pencils, paper, computer, printer, etc.

    f.   Select appropriate music. For most learning styles, music that is instrumental is best for learning. This prevents one from using part of the brain to sing along instead of being focused on the topic at hand. For the auditory or musical learner, music can be especially powerful as subject material can be tied to the music for better understanding and recall.

2.   Create a schedule for study. Determine what topics will be covered by your test and how many days you have to study for the exam. Plan out what topics you will study each day in order to be prepared for the test. Do not plan on studying any new material the night before the exam, as cramming is never a good option. Be sure to devote more time to topics that are unfamiliar or difficult.

3. Use a timer. Set your timer for 20 or 25 minutes. Studies show that the optimal time to study is in 20 to 25 minute segments with a 5 to 10 minute break between each. Your brain is actually best at remembering the first and last thing that you study. Therefore these short segments give you more first and last items. These short segments are short enough to maintain attention (even for those with ADD or ADHD) and long enough to study a substantial amount of information. During your break get up and move around. Be sure your whole body is involved. The physical activity keeps your blood flowing and gives your brain a chance to take a break, without shutting down completely.

4. Study in "chunks". As we mentioned earlier your brain is great at remembering the first and last items on which you focus attention. Use this fact to your advantage by breaking information into lists or chunks of 3 to 5 items. This allows for more first and lasts in the set of information and uses your brains built in systems to your advantage.

5. Concentrate. It seems like the simplest advice, but the importance of concentration cannot be overstated. Concentration is the self-discipline of studying. Studying is not a passive skill (as much as all students wish it was). Studying is an active sport. You must engage your brain. If you struggle with concentration or suffer from ADD / ADHD consider removing anything that might distract you. For this author this meant going to the top floor of the library where the "quite rule" was strictly enforced, finding an enclosed study area where there were no visual distractions, and putting earplugs in so that not even the turning of pages could distract me. It soon became apparent that an hour spent in this environment was far more productive than 2 or 3 hours trying to study in a dorm room or even a more social area of the

library. Do not be afraid to do what it takes to make concentration easier, it is a difficult discipline to build.

6. DO NOT use a highlighter when studying. A highlighter may be beneficial in marking items to be studied at a later time, but that is precisely what makes it such a poor tool for studying. The best use for a highlighter is in a fast paced lecture when something needs to be noted for later study. However, when studying as an individual the highlighter often serves as a mark of procrastination. Instead of highlighting the text to come back to later, take the time to devote it to memory. If the information is too in-depth or is a bit off topic, make a note on a separate piece of paper to come back and study further. The simple act of writing it down instead of highlighting begins the learning process. Make every attempt to understand and process information before moving along to another topic and instead of highlighting for later study.

7. Create connections. The more you can connect a new concept to something you already know the better your learning and recall will be. For visual learners, these connections should be drawn in pictures, flow charts or graphs. For the kinesthetic learner, as much as possible, the connections should be acted out or put into motions.

8. Use all of your senses. As much as possible try to engage all of your senses when studying. It is understood that your sight is always part of studying. Include your speech (which we know is not a true sense) and hearing in your study. Instead of just reading material silently "in your head", read it out loud. This engages three aspects of your brain: sight, hearing, and speech which makes it more likely you will

remember the content. If there is a way you can integrate the whole body into the concept then do so.

9. Study items from broad concepts to minor details. As you begin to study, tackle the major points first. If you understand how whole chapters relate to one another then adding the smaller details will be easier.

10. Always focus on the bold print or italicized words in a text, as these are strong indicators of important material.

11. When you study consider using the same pen / pencil for all study related to this test and then take this pencil with you to the testing center. As you study play a mental trick on yourself by storing all the answers you write into your pencil. With that pencil with you at the exam, you have already written all the answers you are going to need. Sure it is a mental trick, but you have actually studied hard and written all the answers you are going to need. The mental trick simply serves as a psychological reminder to this fact.

12. Use flash cards. Sometimes there is information that simply must be devoted to memory (formulas, historical events, lists, vocabulary). For this type of information use flash cards. Three by five index cards work well. Put the definition or name of the formula on the front of the card and the answer on the back. Quiz yourself using the cards and reviewing the cards you missed in each set before attempting to work through the entire deck again. Flash cards work great for reviewing materials when you only have a few moments (perhaps between classes, or waiting in line).

13. Use mnemonic techniques to memorize materials. There are several mnemonic techniques that work well depending on the situation.

a. For key words or lists consider using an ACRONYM to remember the list. An acronym is an invented combination of letters. If you have ever had the pleasure of playing a musical instrument you probably remember your grade school music teacher saying Every Good Boy Does Fine in an effort to help you remember the order of the notes on the clef scale.

b. Another option for lists or key words is the ACROSTIC - You probably remember Please Excuse My Dear Aunt Sally from grade school when your teacher used it to help you remember the order of operations: Parenthesis, Exponents, Multiply, Divide, Addition, Subtraction.

c. Location method – this method involves using a specific location to tie concepts together. For this example let us assume we are trying to memorize the following short list of landforms: hill, mountain, plateau. We might picture our living room and imagine that as we walk in the door we are met immediately by a hill we must crawl over, followed by a television displaying a picture of the mountain. Lastly sitting there on the sofa is a plateau (you may even picture your uncle who has the flat buzz cut to help you remember the flat plateau). The more vivid you make the pictures the better and easier to remember them they will be.

d. Rhyming Method – This is a two-step method in which you create words that rhyme with numbers and then build an association with those words. This method works best for ordered lists. For example if you were going to remember the following items for a grocery list: milk, bread, eggs, cheese, and chicken. To remember the first item on the list we would find a word that rhymes with "one". For our case, we will choose "run". You are going to picture yourself running and carrying a gallon of milk. Much like the Location method, the trick to making this particular mnemonic device work is to make the picture and relationship between the two words as vivid as possible. So instead of just picturing yourself running with a gallon of milk in hand, you will picture yourself running while pouring the milk over your head. You could even get some of your other senses involved by imagining the smell of the milk to be putrid due to the hot weather in which you are running. By involving more senses and making the picture more vivid you are far less likely to forget the milk when you arrive at the store. This process would be repeated using the next number in the sequence and so on for each item that needs to be memorized.

14. Study groups – If you are a social learner then you will certainly benefit from the advantages that study groups offer. However, be prepared when you arrive and do not expect the study group to replace individual effort needed to learn new material. Study groups typically work best, for both social and solitary learners as a place to test knowledge. By quizzing one another, students can become more confident about material they know and find out what concepts may need a bit more attention. In addition, study groups can often help the student who is stumped on a particular concept. Do not be afraid to ask for study group members to explain something or help you understand it more clearly. Often hearing something described in different words is just the key our brain needs to unlock the information fully.

Scheduling Your Test

It may seem like a simplistic reminder, but if you are a morning person you will want to schedule your exam for the morning hours. Be sure to give yourself adequate time to get up, get ready and face any traffic on your way to the testing center. If you are better in the evenings, schedule the time that is near the end of the day but NOT the last session. Think back to elementary school and the fear of being the last person to turn in their test while others waited for you. You do not want the added stress of those around you leaving while you needlessly fear being the only person left.

Last Minute Preparation for Testing

You have studied as much as possible and tomorrow is the big day. What should you do tonight to make sure you are prepared for the big test? Let us begin with the on thing you should NOT do. Do not get caught up in cramming or even reviewing one last time. It is actually too late for that to do you much good. Tonight you should relax and focus on just a few items.

1. Get to bed early (or at least not excessively late) so you will be fresh for your test.

2. Use this time for positive self-talk. Remind yourself how much you have studied for this exam and how prepared you are to show just how well you know the information.

3. The night before set out the items you will need for testing. Lay out clothing you plan to wear (go for comfort over style here). Make sure you include a jacket / hoodie as most testing centers tend to stay cold to help you stay awake. In addition, be sure your photo ID, pencils, calculator, and other requirements for the test are ready to be grabbed as you walk out the door.

4. Eat breakfast. Sure this is motherly advice, but it is good advice. Your brain needs fuel to function. Make sure you feed it. Avoid sugary foods that will leave you in a

slump later and impact concentration levels. High protein foods are best as they help provide long-term energy.

5. Visit the restroom 15 – 20 minutes before the test and refrain from drinking fluids within an hour of your test.

6. Arrive 10-15 minutes early for the test so you do not have the stress of being late.

7. During the last few minutes, it is okay to review a formula or fact sheet of information you have dedicated to memory. One of the first things you will do when you sit for the exam, is to "dump" this information onto your scrap paper. Note that this is not the time to "cram" this information into your brain. It should already be memorized; you are just reviewing one last time.

8. Before you are seated for the exam, take a few deep breaths and relax. If you are subject to test anxiety we will cover more on how to relax a bit later.

Test-Taking Tips

When we began this text we explained that taking a test was much like a sport and that understanding the rules of the game (test-taking skills) were just as important as ability to play (subject matter knowledge). In the next several pages we are going to explore ways you can put the rules of the game to work for you. By understanding and applying these test-taking strategies you improve your odds for success.

The number one tip for taking a test is to **remain confident**. It is amazing how confidence can change the outcome of situations. If you have studied adequately your hard work will pay off when it comes to taking the test. Just relax and trust yourself. If you suffer from test anxiety this tip is even more important. (See also the tips for test anxiety a few pages later.)

Once you begin the test and the timer begins, **take the first few moments to write down any formulas, dates, facts that you have dedicated to memory**, but are not included on a "fact sheet" for the exam. Doing this "brain dump" allows your brain to figuratively free up space that was being used to hold this information. It also ensures you do not forget the information later down the road when you need it.

Before you begin, take a look at the entire test and determine how you will **budget your time**. Often tests are computerized so this does not mean to click through every question, but simply learning how many questions there are so that you can stay on target to finish in the time allotted.

It often goes without saying, but it should not, that you need to **read the instructions**. You have probably had that teacher that gave you the following directions test that asked you to read the whole test before marking any answers and the result likely resulted in hilarity as your classmates did silly things because they didn't read the directions. (You would never fall for that trick yourself). While this is not elementary school and a standardized test is not going to set out to confuse you with directions, they are no less important. The difference between understanding mark the "best" answer and "only" answer can save you a great deal of confusion, and the difference between writing an essay about all of the topics or choosing a topic can mean the difference in passing and failing. So as elementary and boring as it is, take time to read the directions.

After reading the directions, you will want to **begin with the easiest questions** first. Most tests today are written in increased order of difficulty so this is typically the way you approach the test anyway. Answering easy questions will serve to boost your self-confidence and prepare you for the harder questions to come. However, if you encounter a problem that "stumps" you do not be afraid to leave it unanswered and return to it at a later time. Be sure you either mark the question on the test or make note on your scrap paper so you do not submit the test with an unanswered question. A question may often have clues to other questions within it.

Life Span Developmental Psychology

As you answer questions **rely on your first impressions** and do not over think the answers. Unless you are 100% sure that you have the wrong answer and are 100% that the answer you are changing to is the correct answer do not deviate from your initial "gut reaction". Teachers would be quite wealthy if rewarded every time a student admitted to changing from a correct to incorrect answer. Do not be that student. Go with your first instincts unless you are absolutely sure you were wrong.

If you finish early, **use the time to review** your answers. Check to be sure you answered all of the questions. Proofread any essays for spelling and grammatical errors. If the test covered mathematics, check your calculations and use the calculator if it is acceptable to do so.

Multiple Choice Questions

Depending on the type of test you are likely to encounter different types of questions. Each of these question types has specific strategies that will help you in taking tests. The most common type of test question for standardized tests is the **multiple-choice** test. Consider these strategies for these types of questions:

1. Before reading the answers to a multiple-choice question try to formulate the answer on your own. This adds confidence to your answer and ensures your brain is engaged in the answering process.

2. While you should formulate your own answer before reading the choices, be sure you read all of the answers before selecting your answer.

3. Statements that begin with concrete exceptions: never, none, always, except, most, least, are likely not the answer.

4. Eliminate unlikely answers. If you can reduce the possible answers to 2 you increase your odds of selecting the right answer or even guessing correctly.

5. If you must guess consider these guidelines:

a. If there are two answers that are opposites from one another then the answer is likely one of those two answers.

b. If there are two answers that are very similar, it is likely that the answer is neither of the two.

c. Typically the longer and more descriptive answer is the correct answer

d. If your answers are numbers then it is likely that the answer lies in the middle of the range of answers, not at the extremes. For example, if you answers are:

a) 100   b) 10   c) 9   d) 0.02

You would eliminate the 100 and .02 and then determine if the answer is either 9 or 10. Again this is not always correct but helps in a situation where you may be forced to guess.

6. Be sure you answer every question. Most tests do not penalize you for guessing so it is best to answer every question even if guessing. Research your specific test for rules about penalties for wrong answers so you know how to approach guessing.

7. Watch out for questions that ask for opposites such as "which of the following is NOT" or "Which statement is false." These questions require reverse thinking.

True / False Questions

While it is not common for Standardized test to have questions other than multiple choice sometimes you may encounter True / False questions. For **True / False** questions consider the following tips.

1. Look at specific details. Specific details tend to make the statement true. For example, The Empire State Building is 1,250 feet tall. The detail of 1250 feet is a very specific detail and chances are this test question is TRUE.

2. When forced to guess, choose TRUE. More questions tend to be true than false, as most instructors and test writers find it more difficult to write statements that are false.

3. Look for extreme words such as: all, always, only, nobody, everybody, absolutely, etc. These words tend be used in statements that are FALSE.

4. Look for qualifying words such as: seldom, often, many, seldom, much, sometimes, etc. These words tend to make the statement TRUE.

5. Look for reasons. If the statement includes a reason it tends to be FALSE. Words like since, because, when, and if add justification or reasoning to the statement and tend to make it FALSE. Also check the justification to make sure it is complete. An incomplete justification makes the statement FALSE.

6. Look for negative words such as: not, none, or no. Also check for negative prefixes such as *un-,im-, miss-*. These negatives can confuse the statement and should be treated with caution.

Matching Questions

Sometimes you will encounter matching questions. These will often appear in a format very similar to multiple choice questions, but should be treated a bit differently. Here are a few tips to help you navigate these types of questions.

1. Read the directions carefully. Sometimes matching answers may be used only once, in other questions the answers may be used more than once. This certainly makes guessing much more difficult if there are answers that can be used more than once.

2. Look at both "sides" or sets of answers / questions. Get an idea of what the relationships might be between the two groups.

3. Use one list to find matches on the second list. This will keep confusion to a minimum.

4. Check the entire second "side" before selecting answers. There may be a more correct answer that follows.

5. Cross off matches on the second "side" in order to make finding subsequent matches easier.

6. Do not make a guess until you have worked through the entire first "side" one time completely.

Overcoming Test Anxiety

One of the most debilitating problems a student can face is test anxiety. Test anxiety can manifest itself through tense muscles, fast heart and breathing rate, cramps, and even nausea. The student who suffers from test anxiety often knows the material as well as, or better than his or her classmates, but this never shows up on tests because the anxiety takes over. It is important for those who suffer from test anxiety to remain calm and confident. There are also other ways to help the brain and body cope with this type of anxiety.

1. **Breathe**. Breathing is not only essential to our existence, but serves as a way of relaxing the mind and body. Purposefully taking a few deep breaths can do a great deal to bring calm to the body. When you feel anxiety about to take over, begin to breath deeply and calmly. Three to five deep breaths normally do the trick and can be repeated as often as necessary.

2. **Relax**. There will be times during the test that you begin to feel anxious. Recognize this feeling. Does it begin with tightening of the shoulders and neck or does it start in your stomach and slowly take over your body? Become aware of the feelings and

the how they start. When you feel that trigger or beginning consciously focus on relaxation. There are many great books and websites dedicated to relaxation techniques. Explore and find one that works best for you.

3. **Take practice tests.** Before you sit for the actual exam, take as many practice exams as you can. Make the surroundings as much like the test center as you can. Give yourself the same time limits, and breaks you will be taking during the exam. The more you can make the practice seem like a test, the more the test will seem like practice. This brings us to the next point.

4. **Think of the test as practice**. This author, once had a student who scored a 32 on a quiz that covered multiplication facts all of which the student had recited the day before. It was apparent the student had become more and more anxious during the exam. As the class was assigned a new worksheet, this student was given the same quiz with one slight change made. At the top of the page, the word "Quiz" was replaced by "Practice". Guess what he made on the "Practice" sheet? You guessed it; he made a 100. Sure it is going to be hard to convince yourself that the test you are going to take at a testing center is really a "Practice" sheet, but there is no reason that you cannot retake the test. Most CLEP and standardized tests allow you to reset for the exam in 6 months (some less). Sure that is a while to wait and you do not want to stress over this test again, but remind yourself this is not the only shot you have at this. Take some of the pressure off of yourself.

5. **Do not panic.** Chances are that if you suffer from test anxiety you are already well acquainted with panic. Simply do not give into it. Force yourself to relax while reminding yourself of your confidence through positive self-talk.

6. **Stay Positive.** Remind yourself of how much you are prepared for this and that a poor exam score only results from many missed questions not one or two.

7. **Stay Realistic.** As we just mentioned one wrong answer does not mean you will fail the exam. Remind yourself that you simply need to pass. No one needs to know your score; you just need to do well enough to pass the exam. As you continue with positive self-talk do not let one or two questions send you into a spiral of self-doubt and more anxiety. Stay realistic about outcomes and your performance.

8. **Take care of yourself.** This is the most often overlooked advice when it comes to test anxiety. Your body is much more likely to respond appropriately if you are treating it appropriately by eating healthy foods and exercising regularly. In addition, regular exercise is shown to reduce stress and is a great way to build up tolerance and coping skills for test anxiety.

As you prepare for your upcoming exam, realized there are no shortcuts to doing well on a test. There is no replacement for knowledge of this subject matter, but hopefully the study skills mentioned here will help you make the most of your time spent studying. As you take the test remember the test- taking skills, as these will help you demonstrate your true mastery of the subject matter. Before you set for the exam and anxiety takes over be sure to put into practice some of the tactics we have mentioned for overcoming anxiety. If you already know what techniques work well for you those techniques will be at your disposal during the test.

Remember that just as the athlete must not only has mastery of the sport but must understand the rules and remain calm under pressure so must you the test-taker. It is important that you master all three skills as each plays a part in your success. You may not be scoring goals, sinking baskets, or serving aces, but you are going to win this game called test-taking. Just remember to have confidence in yourself.

Chapter 1: Introduction to Lifespan and Developmental Psychology

Overview:
There are a multitude of reasons to study Developmental Psychology. Among these reasons, seeking to understand the different needs of patients and learning how to be self-reflective are among the most important. In addition, Developmental Psychology will help you to become a better nurse by providing you with an understanding of the different psychological, emotional, and physical needs of patients. Of equal importance is the ability to be self-reflective to understand your personal life stage and what motivates you, which will also aid in your understanding of patients.

In this chapter, the general concepts of each stage of the lifespan will be explained chronologically. These concepts will help you to build a basic foundation to the various schools of thought in psychology. It is vital to absorb and remember the information presented in this chapter, as it will be presented throughout your studies of the lifespan. There are many important concepts, most of which have been outlined in **bold**.

Objectives:
By the end of this chapter, you should be able to recognize, understand, and explain the following:

- The domains of development
- The various contexts in which development occurs
- The major theories of developmental psychology and the people associated with them

Developmental Psychology: The Basics:
Psychologists previously thought that development ceased after adolescence. Now, it is well known that thought development continues from birth to death. The process and everything which occurs between birth and death is termed: **lifespan.** The longest period of time a member of a species can live is the **maximum lifespan**: In humans, the maximum lifespan can be as long as 120 years. More frequently, lifespan is thought about in terms of **average lifespan**, which is the average age reached by the members of a given population. The average lifespan can be different for males and females, as well as between cultures and geographic locations. **Life expectancy** is the number of years an individual is expected to live. The overall lifespan of humans is divided into eight categories:

1. Prenatal: conception to birth

2. Infancy: birth- 2 years old
3. Early Childhood: 2 -5 years old
4. Middle Childhood: 6 -11 years old
5. Adolescence: 12 -18 years old
6. Early Adulthood: 19 -34 years old
7. Middle Adulthood: 35- 64 years old
8. Late Adulthood: 64 years old and up

In addition to these categories, death and the dying process are part of the lifespan and need to be studied accordingly. The ages in the above categories are not rigid, but are general guidelines to help divide the lifespan into ages.

Domains of Development:

In Developmental Psychology, three main perspectives are used and best studied when broken into their respective components:

1. **Biosocial Domain:** the combination of the studies of the brain and body changes ("bio") with societal influences ("social"). This combination can be seen in the dilemma concerning how access to adequate nutrition affects physiological development. This dilemma combines concepts related to socioeconomic status/societal influences with biological concepts. The result of this dilemma is: If a child does not have access to fresh fruits, vegetables, and other healthy foods, this child may have stunted growth and a myriad of other health problems.
    a. **Potential Development:** the maximum a child could grow and develop in ideal conditions
    b. **Actual Development:** how much a child actually grows and develops
2. **Cognitive Domain:** Deals with the areas of cognition, such as thought, perception, language, and other mental activities. Researchers in this field would ask such questions as: How do children acquire language and how is perception influenced throughout development?

3. **Psychosocial Domain:** The combination of personality, emotions, relationships ("psych"), and societal influences ("social"). A researcher may ask the question: How can individuals interact with society throughout development?; Or they may study how

interactions throughout the lifespan cause changes in individual psychological development.

Perspectives and Issues in Developmental Psychology:

The following are important perspectives to consider while studying Developmental Psychology:

1. *Change is multidimensional.* There are a multitude of changes that can occur within an individual simultaneously; these changes include physical, emotional, psychological, and more. These changes can affect one another, either lessening or increasing the effect of each change.

2. *Change occurs in many contexts.* An important and often-forgotten aspect of nursing is to not just treat the disease, but to treat the patient. Patients have complex personal histories, economic issues, cultures, languages, and beliefs, all of which influence how a patient responds to care. Many nurses, especially in present culture, forget the impact of being culturally sensitive and it can positively impact the care of their patients.

3. *Developmental Psychology is NOT just about psychology:* Development occurs biologically, sociologically, psychologically, and in more areas, which are affected by education, economic status, religion, and culture.

4. *Change occurs throughout the lifespan:* With the recent understanding that development occurs throughout life, it is apparent each stage of the lifespan has its own milestones and concerns. The term **plasticity** refers to the brain's ability to be able to learn, grow, and develop.

Development in Context:

Developmental change occurs in many different contexts. There are a few important contexts to be familiar with to understand Developmental Psychology:

1. ***Historical context:*** As is implied by the name, this context takes into account the time period during which a person is developing. Growing up in the last twenty years is different than growing up in the 1940s. For example, a woman growing up in today's culture would have different goals and opportunities than a woman growing up in the 1950s. People who were born during the same era, culture, and location generally have similar growth and developmental experiences, referred to as an **age cohort.**

2. ***Socioeconomic context:*** The term **socioeconomic status (SES)** is a termed frequently used in psychology and other similar fields. SES encompasses more than just

financial status: It encompasses education level, income, geographic residence, and employment. These components affect the other components, as they influence how a person grows and develops. The opportunities for an individual from a lower status may be different than the opportunities for someone from a higher class. As such, an individual from a lower socioeconomic status may have more health problems and difficulty finding a well-paying job. There is, also, an extreme prejudice against individuals from a lower class.

3. *Cultural and ethnic contexts:* Culture includes the values, attitudes, customs, and beliefs which have been passed down and maintained in their society over time. Ethnicity is closely tied to culture and includes a shared belief system, ancestry, and religion. Generally speaking, individuals of various ethnic groups can share a single culture while maintaining their own culture within a larger context. This perspective seeks to address a myriad of issues and concerns through the lens of cultural understanding.

4. *Individual and social context:* This context looks at how society affects the individual and vice versa. There are two factors which affect development, internal and external factors. **Internal factors** include: genetics, physical development, and thought. **External factors** include: society, developmental context, or the events occurring during a particular period of development. Internal versus external factors center on the debate of nature (internal factors) and nurture (external factors).

Approaches to Development:

There are three main approaches researchers take when thinking about development:

1. **Continuous Development:** *used by behavioral theorists.* Examines how change depends entirely on the environment, is slow, and constant. Change is due largely to rewards and punishments.

2. **Overlapping Stages:** *used by psychosocial theorists.* There are stages of distinct change between Continuous and Discrete Development, which are dependent on environmental, genetic, and inherited factors.

3. **Discrete Stage:** *used by psychoanalytic and cognitive theorists.* Examines how change is entirely dependent on a person's age and is the result of genetic forces which are affected by the environment (predisposition). These theorists also believe change only occurs at particular times.

Using an Ecological Approach:

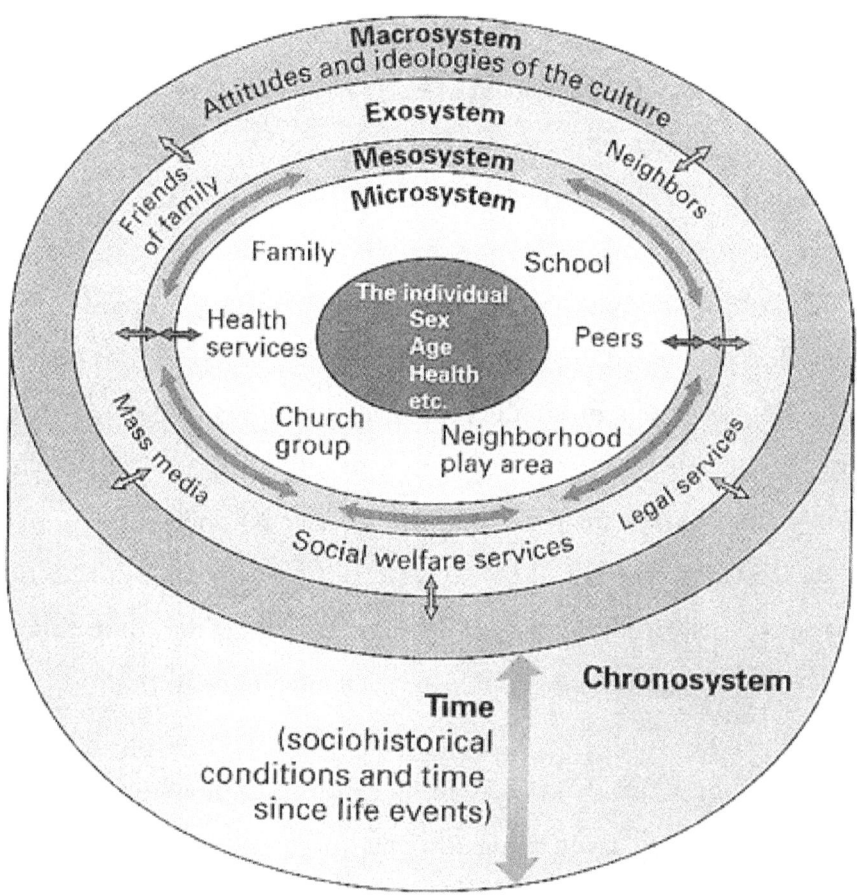

The diagram above is the conventional pictorial representation of how the *Ecological Model* works. This model was first proposed by **Urie Bronfenbrenner**. The diagram is made of concentric circles surrounding the individual person, located in the middle. The circles closest to the individual have the most influence on them, while those farther away have less of an influence.

The **microsystem** is the first layer surrounding the individual and is comprised of the factors which directly influence an individual. Such influencing factors can be: family, school, or peers. The individual systems are connected by **mesosystems.** These systems do not contain influences. The **ecosystem** contains the distant entities which have less of an effect on the individual, such as neighbors, media, and family friends. The outer layer is the **macrosystem,** which is comprised of the broad ideas of the overall culture in which people live and thrive. Affecting each of the subsystems is time, which is contained within the **chronosystem.** There is overlap between the different systems.

Theories of Developmental Psychology:

There are four theories, or 'schools of thought', found in all of psychology, even in developmental psychology. Each theorist views development through a different lens. Understanding the theories and how they differ is vital to building a foundation in Developmental Psychology. The 'schools of thought' are: Psychoanalytic Theory, Behavioral Theory, Cognitive Theory, and Humanistic Theory.

1. **Psychoanalytic Theory:** A significant name in psychoanalytic theory is **Sigmund Freud,** who was a medical doctor and the founder of psychoanalysis. He divided the mind into three levels: the **conscious mind**, the **preconscious mind**, and the unconscious **mind.**

    i. **The Conscious Mind**: a small part of the mind which includes active and easily- recalled experiences.

    ii. **The Preconscious Mind:** this part of the mind falls under the conscious mind and includes memories that can be recalled, despite not actively occurring in thought.

    iii. **The Unconscious Mind:** A 'storage area' for instinctual desires, needs, past thoughts, and memories. Even though they may not be actively recalled, they are a driving force of an individual's behavior.

Freud believed some of the items stored in the **unconscious mind** were inaccessible because they had been **repressed**. Repression is one of the many **defense mechanisms** which Freud proposed--ways the mind protected itself from unpleasant memories, ideas, or thoughts.

Life Span Developmental Psychology

Defense Mechanism	Definition	Example
Repression	Blocking a threatening memory from the consciousness	Children from abusive homes may not remember the specific abuse
Displacement	Placing hostile feelings onto objects other than the source of the feelings	A child who is upset about a new baby coming home and cuts the hair off of dolls or breaks them apart
Rationalization	Justifying a failure with a socially acceptable reason instead of the actual reason	Someone refusing to drink, and instead of saying they prefer not to drink. Giving an alternate excuse to avoid harassment of peers.
Reaction Formation	Changing feelings of anxiety into their opposite in 'real life'	Someone who is uncertain about their religious faith may become evangelical and try to convert their peers
Regression	Going back to an earlier state of behavior	A previous only child who no longer sleeps with a blanket or favorite toy begins to do so again after a new baby arrives
Denial	Refusing to admit that something upsetting exists	A parent is told her child is cutting school but the parent refuses to believe it.

Life Span Developmental Psychology

Freud also developed a new way to organize the personality within the framework of the conscious, preconscious, and the unconscious. He believed there were three main parts within the personality of an individual: **the id, the superego,** and **the ego.**

> **The id:** The first component present within the personality. Present at birth and is completely an unconscious component. The id controls the biological desires for food, sleep, water, and sex. It is not realistic and has no concept of reality, possibility, or time.

> **The superego:** Also called "morality." According to Freud, the superego is what causes people to feel guilt. The superego and the id are at odds, demanding the individual does the "right thing. This dilemma is what causes a person to feel guilty about desiring the bodily pleasures, which the id craves. The superego remains in the preconscious area of the mind.

> **The ego:** This is the mediator between the carnal desires of the id and the 'hyper-morality' of the superego. The ego functions as a reality check and helps to plan, remain rational, and mediate desires. This mediation helps the individual to find socially acceptable ways to satisfy the id. The ego moves throughout the conscious, preconscious, and unconscious mind.

Freud's Theory of Psychosexual Development:
According to Freud, personality develops based on changes in the **libido,** or life force, which is analogous to sexual energy within a person. The libido begins at birth and is completely done developing by age five. Freud also believed that if an individual did not move through the stages of the lifespan appropriately, then they would become 'stuck.' He did not use the term 'stuck', though. Rather, he dubbed the issue 'fixated.' The fixations one experienced would affect their personal development. Below are the stages of psychosexual development. Keep in mind that libido is analogous to sexual energy, though they are not necessarily the same idea. If fixation occurs at any stage, anxiety results, thus triggering defense mechanisms.

Life Span Developmental Psychology

Stage	Age	Characteristics	Fixation
Oral Stage	Birth to 1 year	Pleasure is derived from oral actions of the mouth: suckling, chewing, and biting	Improper weaning will lead to oral fixation. Fixation may manifest as nail biting, overeating, smoking, or gum chewing
Anal Stage	1-3 years	Satisfaction is derived from the anus and defecation, as well as repetitive actions (more often the case)	Improper toilet training and a lack of a structured routine can lead to anal fixation. Generally manifests as a controlling personality, often referred to as "anal-retentive"
Phallic Stage	3-6 years	The discovery of the genitals: can lead to envy of the opposite gender	Improper education and lack of parental involvement can lead to misplaced sexual feelings for the opposite gender and the conflict of not having the opposite genitals may lead to fixation on the matter
Latency Stage	7-11 years	No significant development occurs. Girls start to play more with girls and boys more with boys	Improper exposure to children of both genders can lead to inadequate knowledge of the opposite gender and the inability to socialize with them
Genital Stage	12 years and up	Sexual experimentation occurs and relationships are sought, generally with the opposite gender	If fixation develops during a previous stage, it will affect the rest of the lifespan. Freud believed that if this were to occur, the individual would become homosexual

During the *Phallic Stage,* a parental obsession may develop. Freud believed that children become sexually attracted to their parent of the opposite sex. For male children, this notion was referred to as the **Oedipus complex**. For female children, this notion was referred to as the **Electra complex**. The name Oedipus refers to a Greek play, *Oedipus Rex* (meaning King Oedipus), written by Sophocles. In the play, the parents of Oedipus are informed shortly after his birth that he will grow up to kill his father and marry his mother. Despite efforts having been made to prevent this from happening, Oedipus grows up to fulfill the prophecy made at his birth. Although much more happens during the play, Freud chose to use the prophecy as the basis for his theory. The Oedipus complex says that male children will grow to feel resentment towards their fathers and have latent desires to marry their mother. The name Electra is derived from another play by Sophocles. During this play, Electra desires to kill her mother while competing with her for the attention of her father.

Successful resolution of these complexes occurs differently for boys and girls. Part of the process for male children is experiencing **castration anxiety.** During this time period, they believe that if their desires for their mother are discovered, their father will retaliate and castrate them. Part of the resolution process for female children is experiencing **penis envy**. During this part of the process, female children realize they do not have a penis, which causes anxiety. Eventually, in most female children, their desire shifts from their father to socially acceptable men. Thus, these complexes are resolved.

Evaluation of Freud's Theories:
Freud established these notions of the Oedipus and Electra complexes without a significant background in Greek literature or Greek mythology. It's important to note that most Greek plays come from Greek mythology and Ancient Greek religion. Though difficult to understand in today's culture, Freud was from a different time with differing views on sexuality and sexual attraction. When studying his viewpoints, a cultural and historical lens is required to fully understand Freud's theories and the intricacies of the complexes.

Many of Freud's theories have been accepted and expanded upon. However, many of his ideals have been rejected and criticized. Notably, his notions of psychosexual development have been widely rejected. Reasons for rejection range from religious differences, lack of sufficient evidence, incomplete studies, and faulty data. Despite his many criticisms and flaws, Freud's work has been instrumental in providing a springboard for future work in personality, adolescent development, and attachment theory.

Two of the most notable people who have based their research on Freud's work are: Karen Horney and Carl Jung. Karen Horney accepted the theory of conflict between parents and a child, but attributed it to parental hostility and intimidation. Carl Jung accepted the notion that people have a conscious mind and a personal unconscious mind, and proposed the notion of a collective unconscious. Jung believed the collective unconscious was present at birth and represented the collective experience of previous generations.

Erik Erikson's Stages of Psychosocial Development:
Erik Erikson was another contributor to the psychoanalytical branch of psychology. According to Erikson, development occurred as a series of conflicts, which needed to be resolved at each stage of life. Unlike Freud, Erikson did not focus on sexuality, but on emotions. Also, unlike Freud, Erikson did not set hard age limits on the life stages of adulthood.

Life Span Developmental Psychology

Below are the life stages according to Erikson:

Age	Stage/Conflict Faced	Characteristics/ Questions Asked	Outcome
Birth to 1 year	Trust vs. Mistrust	Infants learn to trust caregivers to supply their needs.	If the child's needs are not met, they will not trust people or the world to help support them.
		"Is the world predictable and supportive?"	If the issue is resolved, the infant will learn to hope.
Age: 2-3 years	Autonomy vs. Shame and Doubt	Toddlers explore independence and must be allowed to start becoming self-sufficient.	If the toddler is not allowed to explore and learn to become self-sufficient, they may grow to doubt themselves.
		"Can I do things by myself or do I need others to help?"	If the child learns they can do things by themselves, they will learn "free/self-will."
Age: 4-5 years	Initiative vs. Guilt	Children learn about the acceptability of their actions. They must have the ability to explore and help with tasks and projects	If the conflict is resolved, the child learns their purpose.
		-"Am I good or bad?"	If their conflict is not resolved, the child will develop feelings of guilt for wanting independence.
Age: 6-11 years	Industry vs. Inferiority	Children learn to accomplish things and want to be productive members of their family/society. -"Am I successful or am I a failure?"	If the conflict is resolved the child learns "competence."
			If the conflict is not resolved, the child may feel inferior.
Age: 12-18 years	Identity vs. Role Confusion	Adolescents need to explore their identity and discover their inner self	If the conflict is resolved, the adolescent will learn a "fidelity" to a particular identity.
		"Who am I and who will I be?"	If the conflict is not resolved, the adolescent may feel conflicted with their role, for the remainder of their life.
Young Adult	Intimacy vs.	Individuals consider relationships	If the conflict is resolved, the

		Isolation	and learn to become intimate (emotionally).	individual learns how to "love,"
			"Will I share my life with someone or be alone?"	If the conflict is not resolved, the individual may become a "loner."
Middle Adulthood		Generativity vs. Stagnation	Adults attempt to create meaningful contributions to leave for future generations.	If the conflict is resolved, the individual learns how to "care."
			"How will I contribute to society?"	If the conflict is not resolved, the individual may fail to leave behind anything meaningful.
Late Adulthood		Integrity vs. Despair	Adults reflect on whether their lives have been fulfilling.	If the crisis is resolved, the adult will learn to feel good about their life and learn "wisdom".
			"Have I lived a full life?"	If the conflict is not resolved, the adult may become depressed about having lived a meaningless life.

2. **Behavioral Theory:**
Behaviorists focus on observable behavior rather than mental processes. **John B. Watson** was an influential behaviorist who postulated that in order for psychology to be a true science, experiments must be able to be performed. Because experiments cannot be performed on intangible objects, focus shifted to observable concrete actions. As such, behaviorism was born.

Classical Conditioning:
One of the facets of behaviorism is **classical conditioning**, which was postulated by **Ivan Pavlov.** Pavlov was a physiologist by profession who studied digestion in dogs. Based on the common knowledge of when an individual feels hunger or thinks about food, they produce more saliva. Pavlov wanted to study saliva production in dogs when exposed to various foods. Through his research, he noticed the dogs would salivate, even before they were presented with food. He soon realized the dogs were associating his presence with food.

Following more observations, Pavlov conditioned his dogs to salivate in response to a bell toll. Every day, he would ring the bell while the dogs were salivating and then present them with food. Eventually, the dogs began to salivate when the bell rung, even if food was not presented.

Important components of classical conditioning:

- **Unconditioned Stimulus (UCS):** food
- **Unconditioned Response (UCR):** salivation
- **Conditioned Stimulus (CS):** bell
- **Conditioned Response (CR):** salivation

Important things to remember:

- **UCR:** usually is a natural reflex
- **Pavlov's bell:** originally a neutral stimulus (had no significance)
- UCR becomes a CR when pairing the UCR with a new stimulus

Classical conditioning pairs a new reflex (involuntary physiological response) with a previously neutral stimulus (a bell), which now has meaning. Despite being useful, classical conditioning is limited due to the fact that only reflexive actions can be used. As such, it is not the optimal way to teach a variety of things. If responses can be classically conditioned, the responses can also undergo **extinction.** For example, if Pavlov's dog were trained with a ringing bell and then were denied food, they would "unlearn" the association of a bell toll meaning food. Hence, the response can be reconditioned.

Another example of classical conditioning is the Little Albert experiment, which was performed by John Watson. In this experiment, a nine-month-old boy was exposed briefly to a white rat, a rabbit, a dog, and monkey masks (with and without hair), cotton wool, and various other items the child had never been exposed to previously. Little Albert was not afraid of any of these items. Before turning one year old, Watson started to condition him. A white rat was placed near Albert and as he reached out for the rat, Watson would make a loud noise which scared Little Albert. The noise was paired with the white rat multiple times until eventually, Little Albert began to cry and show fear when the write rat was brought into the area. Little Albert now associated the white rat with the loud noise and feared the rat.

- **UCS:** loud noise
- **UCR:** fear/crying
- **CS:** white rat (previously a neutral stimulus)
- **CR:** fear/crying

After the experiment, Little Albert showed **stimulus generalization** to all furry white objects, not just the white rat. He was also afraid of white cotton, a fake Santa beard, a white rabbit, and a sealskin coat.

Operant Conditioning:
A different aspect of behaviorism is **operant conditioning**, which was postulated by **B.F. Skinner.** He developed this notion in response to the failings of classical conditioning. Skinner believed learning occurred due to **selective reinforcement**, or reinforcing certain behaviors while not reinforcing (or even punishing) other behaviors.

- **Reinforcement:** any action or condition which *increases* the probability of a behavior occurring again.

- **Punishment:** any action or condition which *decreases* the probability of a behavior occurring again.

- **Positive:** if reinforcement or punishment *introduces* something. If the introduced stimulus is pleasant, it reinforces the desired behavior. However, if the stimulus is unpleasant, it punishes the behavior.

- **Negative:** if a reinforcement or punishment *removes* something. If the removed stimulus is unpleasant, it reinforces the behavior. If the removed stimulus is pleasant, it punishes the behavior.

For example, if you are attempting to get your child to clean her room for an entire week and you want to positively reinforce the behavior, introduce something pleasant, or remove an unpleasant task to negatively reinforce the good behavior, such as removing a chore. However, if the room is not clean by the end of the week, the child could be punished by adding something unpleasant, such as a chore, or the parent could remove something pleasant, like TV privileges.

For punishment to be successful, it must occur directly after the undesirable behavior occurs. If it is not administered directly after the undesirable behavior, it will not be paired with the correct behavior. The association of a bad behavior and punishment will not be made.

Reinforcement Schedules:
When reinforcing behavior, frequency matters as much as what is done or not done. There are five schedules of reinforcement: continuous, fixed ratio, fixed interval, variable ratio, and variable interval.

Schedule	Definition	Pros	Cons
Continuous	Behavior is rewarded every time it is performed	Good for initial learning	Difficult to maintain
Fixed Ratio	Behavior is rewarded after it is performed a certain number of times	Rapid response of desired behavior	Difficult to maintain
Fixed Interval	Behavior is rewarded after a specified number of minutes pass		Low success rate
Variable Ratio	The desired behavior will occur a random number of times before it is rewarded	Easy to maintain, which produces a high and steady response rate	
Variable Interval	The desired behavior will be rewarded after a random timeframe has passed	Easy to maintain Low and steady response rate	

Social Learning Theory:

A different learning theory, which was postulated by **Alfred Bandura,** stated there was a difference between learning and behavior. Bandura believed learning can happen from observing others and reinforcement is not always necessary for learning to occur. His most famous study was the Bobo Doll study. A Bobo doll, an inflatable doll which is weighted on the bottom, was often used as a child's toy during Bandura's experiments. A group of children was allowed to view videos of other children beating up the Bobo doll. Some children were rewarded for their action, others were punished, and the rest were given no reaction. After viewing the video, the children were allowed to play with their own Bobo doll. The children who had seen violent behavior rewarded, were quick to mimic the violent behavior. The group of children that had seen the video of children being punished for beating up the doll were resistant to mimicking the punished behavior. The children who had seen the video of other children beating up the doll and receiving no reaction, were okay with mimicking the violent behavior. Bandura believed this experiment showed how children learn by observation.

3. **Cognitive Theory**

Much like Erikson's stages of development, **Jean Piaget's** theory contained stages of cognitive development.

Stage	Age	Description
Sensorimotor	Birth to 2 years	-Children learn by using their senses -Children repeat actions multiple times, trying to understand if the world is consistent Ex. A child throws a toy or food on the floor repeatedly, testing gravity
Preoperational	2-7 years	-Children learn "operations", or the ability to manipulate objects -They understand symbolic functions or that one object can stand for another Ex. A banana can be used as a telephone
Concrete Operational	7-11 years	-Children can engage in more complex thoughts and behaviors -Concrete refers to *tangible* objects -They Understand more about cause and effect
Formal Operational	11 years and beyond	-These adolescents and adults can understand logical and abstract thoughts -They have the ability to think hypothetically and into the distant future Ex. Not doing a homework assignment can have larger consequences than a bad grade on the assignment

After his initial theory, Piaget added another stage for adults who had completed a college or graduate education, **Post-Formal Operational Stage**. This stage comes with the ability to combine and utilize more than one abstract idea at the same time.

Piaget's theory has been criticized for a variety of reasons:

- Underestimated the abilities of preschoolers
- Overestimated those in the formal operational stage
- Children may not move fluidly through the stages
- Influences of culture are not taken into account

Lev Vygotsky:
Vygotsky was another cognitive theorist who focused more on the social aspect of cognitive development than Piaget. Vygotsky believed language was a vital part of learning. One of his most important contributions was his idea of **zone of proximal development (ZPD).** This idea of ZPD held that the best way to help someone learn was to balance previous knowledge with un-acquired knowledge.

For example: A child may be able to read simple books independently, while more complex books are too difficult. The child's ZPD lies between the two extremes, with books a child can read with the help of a parent or teacher.

Information Processing and Memory:

Cognitive theorists view the brain as a computer with encoded information. This encoded information is put into a format which can be stored or retained appropriately and then retrieved from memory. There are three main categories of memory:

1. *Sensory Memory:*
   - Lasts a few seconds
   - Holds information from the senses (hearing, taste, touch, smell, sight)
   - Information will leave this area if not rehearsed/repeated to be stored more permanently

2. *Short-term Memory:*
   - Limited capacity of 5-9 items, referred to as **Miller's Magic Number**
   - The brain has the ability to organize items into groups to allow for more storage

3. *Long-term Memory:*
   - Unlimited capacity and unlimited duration
   - Information stored here must undergo a rehearsal strategy
   - Information can be retrieved with **retrieval strategies**

   Retrieval Strategies:
   - **Rehearsal:** repeating something until it is remembered
   - **Elaboration:** beginning with simple information and growing to more complex ideas/thoughts
   - **Association:** connecting new information with older information
   - **Retrieval Cues:** a physical, verbal, visual, or auditory cue to aid in remembering

Another type of memory is called **Working Memory**: where we hold information currently in use.

4. **Humanistic Theory:**

Abraham Maslow, another psychologist, believed that development occurred due to two types of motivation, intrinsic and extrinsic.

Intrinsic Motivation: how an individual feels about completing an action and it gives them motivation to complete the action.

Ex. Exercising makes the body feel well; the end result of feeling better is motivation for individuals to work out.

Extrinsic Motivation: an external reward is presented to an individual to complete an action. This external reward gives motivation.

Ex. Continuing to work a boring job due to the external motivation of receiving a paycheck. Maslow's significant contribution to humanistic psychology was his notion of the Hierarchy of Needs.

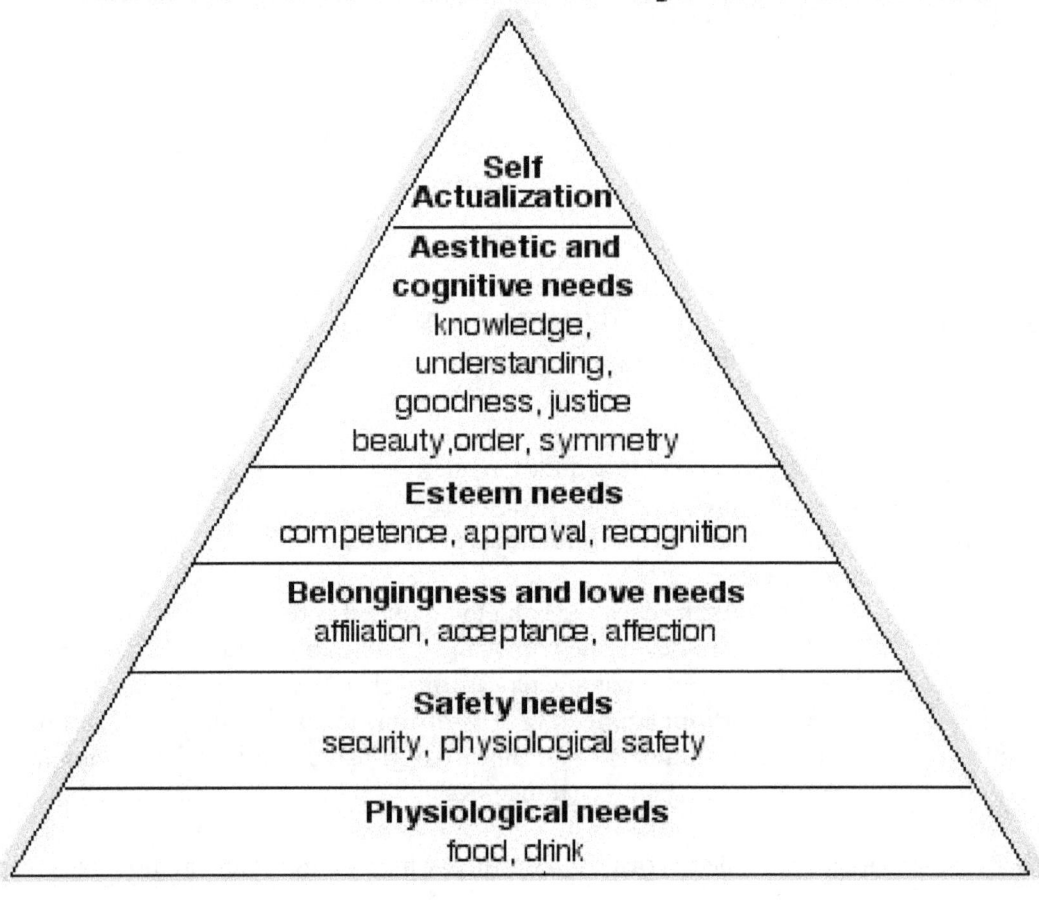

- **Deficiency Needs:** When a specific set of needs are missing, an immediate response is prompted. These needs include: physiological, safety, belonging, and self-esteem.
- **Basic Needs:** Needs that must be met prior to moving on to the next stage of the hierarchy.
- **Psychological Needs:** belonging, self-esteem, and self-actualization
    - **Self-Actualization:** the need to nurture the self to achieve maximum potential

Another prominent humanistic psychologist, **Carl Rogers**, believed people have the capacity to change and improve themselves as long as someone believes in them. Rogers postulated the notion of **unconditional positive regard.** Regardless of someone's actions, an individual would still approve of another individual who has committed poor actions.

Ex. If a close friend is smoking, an individual may disapprove of the unwise behavior, but still love the individual committing the behavior.

Life Span Developmental Psychology

Chapter 1: Review

1. Perception and language are part of the:

    a. Biosocial Domain

    b. Psychosocial Domain

    c. Cognitive Domain

    d. Humanistic Domain

2. Socioeconomic status includes:

    a. Age

    b. Income

    c. Genetics

    d. Personality

3. A child refuses to let his father help tie his shoes, despite the fact that the child had been trying to tie his shoes for fifteen minutes, unsuccessfully. According to Erikson, what stage is the child in?

    a. Integrity vs. Despair

    b. Industry vs. Inferiority

    c. Autonomy vs. Shame and Doubt

    d. Generativity vs. Stagnation

4. Every time someone flushes the toilet, the shower water becomes hot, causing the individual to jump backwards. Over time, the person begins to jump back automatically after hearing a toilet flush, even before the water temperature changes. What is the unconditioned stimulus?

    a. Jumping back

    b. The 'flush' noise

    c. Hot water

5. A father gives his child a credit card at the end of their first college year as a reward for good grades. As a result, the child's grades continue to improve the second year. What type of conditioning and reinforcement is this?

a. Classical/Negative

b. Operant/Positive

c. Operant/Negative

d. Classical/Positive

6. Jane's mother has two crackers, both of equal size. The mother breaks one of the crackers into four pieces. Jane, wanting the most, grabs all four pieces even though the pieces and whole cracker are equal. Jane's choice illustrates Piaget's concepts of:

a. Egocentrism

b. Concrete Operations

c. Conservatism

d. Humility

7. Who was the developmental theorist who proposed the idea of **unconditional positive regard?**

a. Erikson

b. Freud

c. Maslow

d. Rogers

8. Which of the following has unlimited storage and duration?

a. Working Memory

b. Sensory Memory

c. Long-Term Memory

d. Short-Term Memory

9. Who postulated the idea of social learning, using a Bobo doll?

a. Piaget

b. Bandura

c. Skinner

d. Maslow

10. Which stage allows adults to solve multiple complex problems, simultaneously?
    a. Post-Formal
    b. Concrete Operational
    c. Preoperational
    d. Formal Operational

Chapter 1 Answers:

1. C
2. B
3. C
4. C
5. B
6. C
7. D
8. C
9. B
10. A

Life Span Developmental Psychology

Chapter 2: Research Methods in Psychology

Overview:
In this chapter, various types of research methods of general psychology and Developmental Psychology will be explored. Understanding the basic premises for research will aid in the collection of complete information for superior patient care. In addition to exploring various types of research, this chapter will also emphasize how to collect and analyze information.

Objectives:
By this end of this chapter, you should be able to recognize, understand, and explain the following:

- The Scientific Method
- Various research methods and their usage in Developmental Psychology
- Methods of selecting a research population
- Research ethics

The Scientific Method:
All research, regardless of the type of field, uses the Scientific Method to collect research information.

The steps of the Scientific Method are:
1. *Formulate a research question*
2. *Develop a hypothesis*
3. *Test the hypothesis by conducting research which confirms or rejects the hypothesis*
4. *Draw conclusions based on your test results*
5. *Publish findings to make your information available*

Methods:
1. **Naturalistic Observation**
    - Observation of individuals in 'real-life' situations
    - Scientist does not influence the situation
    - Limitations: inability to link cause and effect or generalize results

- Example: Parent and child interactions are recorded via videotape with parental consent. The child does not know they are being observed. The scientist analyzes the tapes after the experiment.

2. **Experiment**
   - Tests a hypothesis in a controlled situation (a laboratory, for example)
   - Can determine cause and effect
   - Utilizes dependent and independent variable
     - **Independent Variable:** a variable that the researcher can change/manipulate
     - **Dependent Variable:** a variable that changes in response to the independent variable
     - **Limitations:** The behavior can be altered and the subjects are aware of being observed, thus experimental bias may occur.
     - **Example:** A researcher wants to determine if caffeine intake affects infant development (hypothesis). Two groups are chosen, an **experimental and control group**. The subjects are randomly assigned to these groups. The experimental group received the treatment (caffeine), while the control group receives no treatment (no caffeine). The control group may be given a **placebo**, or 'fake' treatment.
       - After the groups are randomly assigned, the researcher will study the effects of caffeine by measuring the heart rate and sleeping patterns of the infants.

3. **Survey:**
   - Researchers ask individuals for information about themselves, a given topic, or their opinions
   - Interviews and questionnaires are the main mediums of conducting surveys
   - May be conducted in person, over the phone, through mail, or via the internet
   - **Limitations:** Individuals may not be truthful or may change their answers based on preconceived notions of what they believe they should say
     - **Example:** The US Census is a survey that the federal government performs every ten years to collect demographic data

4. **Interview:**
    - A type of survey that is conducted face-to-face or over the phone
    - **Limitations:** Individuals may not wish to answer certain questions about sex, drugs, or other illicit behaviors
        - **Example:** Elderly women may not want to answer these sorts of questions and may change their answers to something more acceptable
5. **Case Study:**
    - Researchers report and analyze a life history, attitudes, behaviors, thoughts, emotions, and actions of a single individual in a given culture
    - In-depth study
    - **Limitations:** expensive, subjects may drop out, move, die, or forget about the study.

Research Designs:
1. *Longitudinal Study*
    a. Involves studying the same group of individuals over a LONG period of time
    b. Researcher can compare a group of people at one age to themselves at a different age
    c. Changes over time are studied
    d. **Limitations:** expensive to conduct; subjects may drop out, move, or chose to leave the study
2. *Cross-Sectional Study*
    a. Compares individuals at various ages
    b. Groups of people in the study are different in age but similar in other aspects
    c. Research is done at one point in time and is likely a snapshot of the population
    d. **Limitations:** difference in populations may not be due to age, and variables are difficult to control
3. *Cross-Sequential*
    a. Combines longitudinal and cross-sectional studies

      b. Starts with a cross-sectional design and then looks at the same group of people over time

      c. **Limitations:** complex and expensive to conduct, requires long-term commitment

Interpreting Study Results:

It is impossible to prove variables are related or that Variable A caused Change B. It is always possible to show a **correlation** exists between variables. A correlation means two or more variables are related and change together in some way. There are three types of correlations: positive, negative, or no correlation.

- **Positive Correlation:** variables change in the same direction
- **Negative Correlation:** variables change in opposite directions
- **No Correlation:** no relation between variables

Despite having a correlation, there is not a guaranteed **causation** between variables. Causation only occurs when one variable causes a change in another variable. For example: ice cream sales on a beach and shark attacks could be said to be positively correlated because their numbers increase simultaneously. However, eating ice cream does not cause shark attacks. Both events occur simultaneously without causing the other variable.

Ethics in Research:

Unlike other sciences, psychology utilizes human beings in research. Such practices often cause ethical issues. As a nurse, ethical issues are not a new matter. Two ethical topics that are constantly present for nurses are: **informed consent** and **privacy**.

- **Informed consent:** The researcher or physician must explain all aspects of the research or treatment to the subject, including the risks and benefits.
- **Privacy:** The subjects and patients need to know any information collected for and about them during the course of the study will remain confidential.

An uncommon term, **deception**, refers to a researcher not telling a subject the complete truth about the study because it may alter the behavior displayed by the subject. To help decrease the bias of being told the entire truth, researchers deceive the subjects. Such deception can cause ethical concerns; however, to preserve the integrity of the study, it is a necessary evil. After the study, participants undergo **debriefing**. During the debriefing, participants learn of the deception and why it was used. They will receive a copy of the study results and how their information will be used and stored.

Chapter 2: Review

1. The first step of the scientific method is:
    a. Test the hypothesis by conducting research
    b. Draw conclusions based on results
    c. Formulate a research question
    d. Publish findings

2. In terms of research methods, the observation of individuals in real-life situations is referred to as:
    a. Experiment
    b. Case study
    c. Variable
    d. Naturalistic observation

3. Important aspects of ethics in research is/are:
    a. Observation
    b. Documentation
    c. Consent and privacy
    d. Generalizations

4. When conducting a survey, which of the following is used:
    a. Interviews and questionnaires
    b. Evidence-based data
    c. Case study results
    d. Placebo

5. A study that compares individuals across various ages is called:
    a. Cross-sectional study
    b. Longitudinal study
    c. Cross-sequential study
    d. Ethical study

6. When interpreting study results and the variables change in the same direction, this is considered:
    a. No correlation
    b. Full correlation
    c. Negative correlation
    d. Positive correlation

7. The US Census is an example of which type of experimental method:
    a. Interview
    b. Hypothesis
    c. Naturalistic Observation
    d. Survey

8. Debriefing is useful to research to help decrease which of the following:
    a. Bias
    b. Privacy
    c. Knowledge
    d. Communication

9. When a researcher does not tell the study subjects the truth about a study, this is termed:
    a. Breach of confidentiality
    b. Deception
    c. Bias
    d. Unethical behavior

10. Cross-sequential studies combine the results of which other study:
    a. Longitudinal
    b. Cross-sectional
    c. Sequential
    d. Both A and B

Chapter 2 Answers:

1. C
2. D
3. C
4. A
5. A
6. D
7. D
8. A
9. B
10. D

Life Span Developmental Psychology

Chapter 3: Genetics, Prenatal Development, and Childbirth

Overview:
This chapter starts the beginning of the developmental cycle. The foundation for an introduction to genetics will be established. Particular genetic diseases which affect development will also be discussed. Further in the chapter, the fertilization of an egg and the development into a fetus, as well as childbirth, are examined. Most of these concepts are medically based, easing students' understanding.

Objectives:
By the end of this chapter, you should be able to recognize, understand, and explain:

- Basic concepts of genetics and the genetic code
- Genetic and chromosomal abnormalities
- Stages of prenatal development
- Teratogens
- Steps of the birthing process

Concepts of Genetics:
Development begins with **gametes**, or sex cells. The male gamete is sperm and the female gamete is an egg. When gametes combine, their genetic material combines to form a **zygote.** The zygote begins dividing from one cell into two, and so on.

Genetic material of all cells is contained within **chromosomes**, which are housed within the nucleus. **Somatic cells**, or body cells, contain 23 pairs of chromosomes. There are 46 total chromosomes. Half of all chromosomes come from the mother and the other half come from the father. Genetic information is transmitted and carried by **deoxyribonucleic acid**, or DNA. All DNA contains the sugar deoxyribose, a phosphate group, and four bases: **adenine (A), thymine (T), guanine (G),** and **cytosine (C).** Bases are organized into pairs: adenine with thymine and guanine with cytosine.

The basic unit of hereditary information is a **gene**. Genes make up the individual segments of chromosomes. Humans have approximately 100,000 genes. Each gene has specific DNA which carries the code from parent to child. There are two special chromosomes called **sex chromosomes**: **X** and **Y chromosomes.** The sex chromosomes are the twenty-third pair of human chromosome. Females have two X chromosomes (XX), while males only have one X chromosome and one Y chromosome (XY). An individual's genetic makeup is comprised of two different components: a **genotype** and a **phenotype**. The genotype is the actual genetic makeup, including dominant and recessive genes.

- **Dominant Genes:** traits/genes which are always expressed
- **Recessive Genes:** genes which are not expressed

Phenotype is the observable traits which can be seen, such as eye color, hair color, and height. Many genes in the genotype are not observable. Unexpressed genes are called **carriers**. Unexpressed genes can be passed on to offspring. Genes can also act together in **gene-gene interaction** or with their environment in **gene-environment interaction**.

Gene-Gene Interaction:

- **Additive:** shows contributions of multiple genes
  - Ex. A tall woman has a child with a short man and the child is of intermediate height
- **Dominant-Recessive:** genes are non-additive and are a 'one or the other' situation
  - Ex. An individual may have a dominant gene for brown eyes but be a carrier for blue eyes. Brown eyes are shown due to being the dominant gene.
- **Incomplete Dominance:** phenotype is not completely controlled by genotype
  - Ex. Red flowers and white flowers produce pink flowers with a variety of pink hues.
- **X-Linked Genes:** genes on the X chromosome can be dominant or recessive and are more common in men
  - Ex. Male pattern baldness is carried on the X chromosome

Gene-Environment Interactions:

The environment has varying effect on genetics. Studying twins, especially identical twins, helps scientists to study information about how environment influences genetics. **Monozygotic,** or identical twins, occur when one fertilized zygote splits into two identical clusters of cells which fully develop. Identical twins have identical genes. **Dizygotic**, or fraternal twins, occur when two eggs are fertilized by two different sperm at the same time. Fraternal twins are no more genetically similar than a brother and sister born by different pregnancies. It is assumed, though not always correctly, that monozygotic twins are more similar than dizygotic twins. The easiest method of studying differences in twins is by studying twins who were separated at birth. Additionally, studying adopted children and comparing their traits to those of their adoptive parents can indicate whether a particular trait is genetically or environmentally- based: nature versus nurture.

Natural selection has an influence on which genes are expressed at a given time. Natural selection states that organisms which are best adapted to their environment will be most likely to survive, thus passing on their genes to the next generation. **Charles Darwin** originally postulated the theory of natural selection. Darwin's study of the Galapagos finches is an excellent example used to better understand natural selection. Within the Galapagos Islands, Darwin noticed there were different finches particular to individual islands. Each type of finch was slightly different; some had long beaks, while others had shorter beaks. After examination, Darwin discovered the beak size and shape corresponded directly to the food available on the different islands. Each type of finch, though stemming from a common ancestor, has developed into a new species which allowed them to survive and reproduce.

Genetic and Chromosomal Abnormalities:
Many abnormalities have negative repercussions for organisms, and humans are no different. Having too many or too few chromosomes can lead to a variety of **syndromes** (a cluster of symptoms which occur together). There are numerous genetic diseases and here are a few of the more well-known ones:

- **Down syndrome:** Also known as **Trisomy 21**. A child with Down syndrome has three copies of chromosome 21, instead of the normal two copies. Most individuals live well into adulthood with this common abnormality. Individuals with Down syndrome have distinct facial features, such as a round face, thick tongue, and slanted eyes. Most individuals have slow development in many areas and a degree of mental retardation. The degree of mental retardation varies widely, as some individuals live on their own, while other require lifelong care. There are a plethora of accompanying diseases and medical issues with Down syndrome.
- **Phenylketonuria:** PKU is an abnormal digestion of the amino acid phenylalanine. Phenylalanine is a necessary amino acid and is found in many foods. PKU is recessive, meaning parents could be carriers and unaware of the gene. Dietary restriction of phenylalanine can reduce symptoms.

- **Huntington's disease:** a dominant disease with an onset in the mid-thirties. Huntington's is a fatal neuromuscular degenerative disease.
- **Kleinfelter's syndrome:** Kleinfelter's syndrome is a sex-linked chromosomal abnormality, causing the individual to have an extra X chromosome (XXY). Males are usually afflicted, rendering them infertile and with a degree of mental retardation. This syndrome is often difficult to diagnose, thus leading to misdiagnosis. **Fragile X syndrome:** As implied by the name, the X chromosome is 'breakable' and pieces can 'fall off'. Fragile X is not a sex-linked abnormality and the severity depends on how much of the chromosome is missing. Typical symptoms include: mental retardation, large head, and large ears.
- **Turner's syndrome:** Turner's is typical to females and presents when a female has only one X chromosome. Individuals with this abnormality usually have learning disabilities and are infertile. In addition, secondary sex characteristics rarely develop and many individuals have a 'webbed' neck.
- **Other sex-linked abnormalities:** Many sex-linked abnormalities are linked to having an extra sex chromosome. With each addition of a sex chromosome (typically the X chromosome), an increased risk of medical, mental, and learning issues occurs.

Due to the advance of science, many genetic abnormalities can be detected. Such detection can extend to individuals who are carriers. If a screening comes back positive for a genetic disease, genetic counseling is typically provided to pregnant women and spouses. Genetics of each parent are an obvious contribution the likelihood of genetic disease occurrence. Another important contribution to the likelihood of occurrence is the age of the mother at conception. The older a woman is when she conceives, the likelihood of genetic abnormalities present in her offspring increases.

Prenatal Development:
There are three stages to prenatal development:
- **Germinal Stage:**
  - First 14 days
  - Zygote travels down the fallopian tube and implants into the uterine wall
  - Zygote divides and differentiates, thus becoming more specialized

- **Embryonic Stage:**
    - 3rd to 8th week of gestation
    - Development of placenta
    - Underdeveloped cardiovascular system begins to function
    - Head begins to take shape
    - **Cephalocaudal** (head to toe) and **proximodistal** (spine to extremities) development occur
    - Differentiation leads to development of three tissue layers:
        - Ectoderm: outer layers
        - Mesoderm: middle layers
        - Endoderm: inner layers
    - Fetal membranes form, including the chorion and amnion
    - Umbilical cord begins forming
- **Fetal Stage:**
    - 9th week until birth
    - Distinguished by humanoid appearance
    - Fetus begins to move
    - Organs begin to 'function' by the end of the 7th month
    - After 24 weeks, the fetus is **viable**, which means there is an increased chance of survival outside of the womb

Teratogens:
Teratogens are any substances, including food, alcohol, or drugs, which can contribute to or cause birth defects. Environmental triggers, such as maternal malnutrition, are also considered to be a teratogen. Below are a few of the more common and serious teratogens.

- **Diseases:**
    - Rubella (a form of measles) was the first recognized teratogen: If the mother has rubella while pregnant, the child may be born deaf, blind, or have cardiac and brain damage.
    - HIV: has no vaccine or cure. It destroys the body's immune system, making the individual more vulnerable to disease. The transmission of HIV from mother to child can sometimes be prevented if the mother knows she is infected.

- **Medicinal Drugs:**
    - A variety of drugs can be detrimental to a fetus, including prescription drugs.
    - Nonprescription drugs can cause birth defects. Such medications can include antacids, aspirin, and diet pills.
    - Consumption of any non-vital medication is highly discouraged during pregnancy.
- **Psychoactive Drugs:**
    - Alcohol, cocaine, cigarettes, heroin, LSD, methadone, and marijuana are a few psychoactive drugs which can retard the growth of a fetus.
    - The fetus can become addicted to drugs and may go through withdrawal after birth.
        - Three or more alcoholic drinks per day can lead to Fetal Alcohol Syndrome (FAS), which is the leading cause of preventable mental retardation in infants. Children with FAS often have slowed growth, learning disabilities, and social anxieties.
- **Low Birth Weight (LBW):**
    - As defined by the World Health Organization (WHO), low birth weight is when an infant weighs less than 5.5 pounds at birth.
    - Causes for LBW include: preterm birth, drug use, stress, exhaustion, and a variety of infections.
    - LBW children are more likely to have infections and are susceptible to anoxia.

Childbirth and Bonding:

The process of childbirth is personal and varies with every person and pregnancy. There are a variety of methods for labor and delivery. Natural childbirth has become a more accepted birthing method. The Lamaze method is training for both parents to help educate them on how to prepare physically and mentally for childbirth. During the last few weeks of pregnancy, the fetus prepares for birth by turning the head towards the cervix. During the first stage of labor, the cervix dilates to ten centimeters. After the first stage of labor, the baby's head moves through the vagina with the face turned up and the body emerges during the second stage of labor.

After the baby is born, the terminology changes from fetus to **neonate** and there are tests to determine the health of the baby. One test is the **APGAR** score. On a **scale of one to ten**, this test assesses heart rate, color (to determine jaundice and oxygen deprivation), muscle tone, reflexes and respiratory effort. Another test, the **Brazelton Neonatal Assessment Scale,** is used to examine behavior (rooting, suckling, crying, etc.) and neurological functioning.

Life Span Developmental Psychology

Chapter 3: Review Questions

1. The term zygote refers to:
   a. Chromosome pair
   b. Sperm cell
   c. Recessive gene
   d. Fertilized egg

2. The digestive system begins its development during which period?
   a. Fetal
   b. Embryonic
   c. Germinal
   d. Uterine

3. Which of the following is a sex-linked chromosomal abnormality?
   a. PKU
   b. Kleinfelter's Syndrome
   c. Huntington's Disease
   d. Sickle cell anemia

4. The XO chromosomal pattern is a characteristic of:
   a. Turner's Syndrome
   b. Down's Syndrome
   c. Fragile X Syndrome
   d. PKU

5. Which of the following may result in slow fetal growth?
   a. Cigarettes
   b. Liquor
   c. Malnutrition
   d. All of the above

6. Cellular differentiation is:
    a. The process by which cells divide
    b. The processes by which cells connect to form tissues
    c. The process by which cells specialize for specific functions
    d. The process by which cells break down waste products

7. During the embryonic period, the outer layer of the embryo is called the:
    a. Endoderm
    b. Mesoderm
    c. Ectoderm
    d. None of the above

8. Critical body functions of a newborn are measured by:
    a. APGAR score
    b. Brazelton Scale
    c. Age of viability
    d. None of the above

9. Blue eyes are an example of a:
    a. Recessive trait
    b. Dominant trait
    c. Genotype
    d. All of the above

10. Which of the following is a fetal membrane?
    a. Chorion
    b. Endoderm
    c. Ectoderm
    d. Mesoderm

Chapter 3 Answers:

1. D
2. B
3. B
4. A
5. D
6. C
7. C
8. A
9. A
10. A

Chapter 4: Infancy and Toddlerhood

Overview:
This chapter will explore the physical, cognitive, and social development of infants and toddlers. Following the framework of exploring the various categories of development (physical, cognitive, etc.) during the stages of the lifespan, this chapter will discuss infancy and toddlerhood.

Objectives:
By the end of this chapter you should be able to recognize, understand, and explain:

- Stages of physical development of an infant
- Development of various reflexes
- Role of nutrition in infant development
- Categories of attachment in children and adults

Physical Development:
Despite newborn children's dependence on others for their basic needs, they come with certain skills ready to further their development. These skills, which aid in development, help a child to survive and thrive. Some of these skills are:

- **Reflexive behaviors:** coughing, blinking, suckling
- **Inherited behaviors:** these include behaviors that are 'programmed' without prior experience
- **Motor skills:** skills learned later in childhood (at around six months of age) include chewing, swallowing, and self-feeding

In infancy, cephalocaudal and proximodistal development continues. The cephalocaudal principle states that infant's development moves from head to feet. An infant will learn to control their head, then eyes, and face before they learn to control their arms, torso, legs, or feet. The proximodistal principle states that infants develop from the center of the body outward. An infant will learn to control muscles in the upper arm, then lower arm, and then the hands and fingers.

The nervous system continues developing in the postnatal period. The neurons (a type of nerve cell) that are present at birth undergo many changes. The axons (neural fibers which carry messages away from one neuron to another) grow longer and the dendrites (neural fibers which receive messages) become more numerous. The connections between neurons grow stronger as the brain grows. There are approximately one hundred billion brain cells present at birth, most of which are immature. Neural connections allow neural cells to become more efficient to process more information, thus enabling the child to learn more skills. The cortex is the last part to fully develop and is needed to control self-regulatory behaviors such as, walking, sleeping, urination, defecation, and eating.

There are physiological states that refer to the arousal of infants. These states are more pronounced during the first few weeks, after a more predictable routine of sleeping and waking occurs. Newborn children sleep for an average of 16 collective hours a day and then settle into about 13 collective hours a day as toddlers.

Motor Skill Development:
Infants learn many skills without formal instruction, such as sitting and crawling. Infants also learn skills through observation, thus human interaction is critical for proper development. Through studies and observations, it has been determined that children who are raised in environments in which they were held or confined often have delayed motor development. In contrast, children who are allowed to practice motor skills develop quicker. For example, children who are held or confined too much do not have a stepping reflex. The stepping reflex is apparent when an infant or toddler is held over a hard surface, such as a floor and the child will typically move their legs as if they were walking or stepping. The stepping reflex is an example of a gross motor skill. Gross motor skills refer to large body movements, while fine motor skills refer to small body movements.

Reflexes:
A reflex is an involuntary response to a stimulus. Reflexes are the first motor skills an infant develops.

There are three main critical reflexes:

- **Breathing reflex:** maintains oxygen levels
- **Suckling reflex:** the actions which enable feeding
- **Rooting reflex:** the action of an infant trying to find the nipple when hungry. Infants can smell the hormones from milk and will root in response to the smell. Rooting is also triggered by the nipple being touched to the top lip, or the cheek being stroked.

There are other reflexes, which are not critical, but useful for survival:

- **Moro reflex, also called 'startle reflex'**
    - Should be brisk, symmetrical and accompanied with crying

- o When an infant is startled, their arms fling out and then are pulled close to their chest. This is an evolutionary reflex designed to help a child not fall from their mother's arms.
- **Babinski reflex**
  - o When an infant's foot is stroked, the big toe will turn in and the rest of the toes will fan out
  - o Typically disappears in the first few months of life
- **Plantar reflex**
  - o Appears later in infancy
  - o When an infant's foot is stroked, the toes flex
- **Tonic neck reflex, also called 'fencing stance'**
  - o When the head is turned to one side, the opposite arm is extended out and the ipsilateral arm curls behind the head
- **Palmar reflex**
  - o Infant grasps anything placed into the palm
- **Swimming reflex**
  - o When lowered into water, an infant automatically holds its breath and will kick, as if treading water

Sensory-Perceptual Development:
- *Sensation:* a stimulus to the sensory system
- *Perception:* mental process or state of being aware of sensory information

A newborn has immature sensation and perception abilities when compared to an adult, but newborns do use all five senses. Newborns also respond to stimuli, such as pain and temperature. Infants cannot verbally communicate how they feel about certain stimuli. Scientists postulate that an infant's suckling patterns change to convey how they feel about certain stimuli. For example, when an infant is exposed to an unfamiliar stimulus, their suckling pattern and rate increases. When exposed to a familiar stimulus, the physiological changes revert to normal.

A newborn's vision and hearing develop more slowly as compared to the newborn's other senses. The vision of an infant is the least developed of their senses due to the lens having a limited ability to change focus. Infants are near-sighted and prefer to look at high contrast images, bright colors, and faces. The abilities to focus both eyes together (**binocular vision**) develops around fourteen weeks. By the time infants are seven to twelve months old, their vision has improved to the capabilities of most adults.

Hearing develops rapidly. It has been established that a fetus can hear and recognize its mother's voice from within the womb. Newborns are able to differentiate the sound of their mother's voice over other voices and prefer her voice. Infants typically prefer human voices over non-human vocalizations. As hearing develops, infants can turn their head towards the source of a sound and let their eyes locate the source as well.

Nutrition:

During the first few months of life, infants grow rapidly and double their birth weight. Children typically cannot digest solid foods before six months of age. Before the introduction of solid foods and beyond, babies depend on breast milk or formula for necessary nutrients and calories. Breastfeeding is recommended for many reasons. Breast milk has more vitamins, minerals, and antibodies than any formula on the market. The most antibody-rich breast milk appears immediately after birth and is called colostrum. Despite the advantage, recommendations, and cost effectiveness of breastfeeding, less than one fifth of babies born in the USA are breastfed for more than six months. However, in most other countries, children are breastfed for several years. According to the WHO, the average age for weaning from nursing worldwide is four and a half years.

The most common nutrition problem among infants is **macronutrient malnutrition.** Macronutrient malnutrition occurs when the total caloric intake is not high enough for the child to thrive and develop. **Marasmus** is the term used to describe severe macronutrient malnutrition, with an infant weighing about sixty percent of the recommended weight. If a child is suffering from marasmus, typically he or she does not grow and develop well and death becomes a significant possibility. Severe protein malnutrition, **kwashiorkor**, is another type of nutrient deficiency. The nervous system is developing rapidly and neurological damage can occur as a result of these deficiencies. Kwashiorkor is the world's leading cause of infant mortality, generally occurring in developing nations. In the USA, micronutrient malnutrition is far more common than protein malnutrition. Iron and calcium are the most common nutrient deficiencies.

Cognitive Development:
According to Piaget, an infant is in the **Sensorimotor Stage** for the greater part of infancy. To understand the word 'sensorimotor', break the word up into two parts: sensory and motor. Sensorimotor intelligence, according to Piaget, develops as a child performs a series of tasks that engage both of their sensory and motor systems. Sensorimotor intelligence begins with reflexes, such as suckling, listening, and grasping. This intelligence becomes more complex as the child grows and develops. Tasks begin to involve objects and people other than the infant. Later, infants begin to recognize patterns and characteristics of objects in their environment. By the time a child is a year old, they are able to engage in **goal-directed behaviors**. These behaviors have an end goal in mind, such as grabbing a toy or moving across the floor.

Piaget answered the question of how children learn to accomplish goal-directed behaviors with the term **schema**. Schema describes how infants form mental models to help them learn. Piaget believed infants learn in one of two ways: either by **assimilation** or by **accommodation**. If an infant uses **assimilation,** they incorporate *new* information into an already established schema and when an infant uses **accommodation** they modify a schema to include new information. An important schema is object permanence. Object permanence involves the awareness of the existence of an object, even if it is out of sight. This notion develops around eight months of age. Another important schema is reversal, which is the notion that an action can be undone.

Another skill that children gain is **perceptual constancy**. This skill involves the understanding that objects remain the same size and shape despite appearance seeming to change due to its location. Before the development of this skill, a child may think an object shrinks as it moves further away, whereas a child who has this skill understands that if an object moves away, it does not change size.

Categorization and pattern recognition starts during infancy. Children younger than six months of age can categorize objects based on size, shape, density, angle, and number. It is believed that children this young can understand and discriminate between similar objects, such as apples and oranges.

Sensory Coordination:
The senses are not used singularly but in tandem with each other to integrate sight, sound, touch, taste, and smell to understand the environment. The ability to integrate all senses to comprehend the surrounding environment is **intermodal perception**. Infants are able to

demonstrate this ability to some extent. An infant may hear a sound and look in the wrong direction when attempting to find the source of the sound. Between three and six months of age, infants begin to correctly match sounds to their sources.

Cross-modal perception is the ability to imagine one sense when using another. For example, passing a favorite restaurant one can imagine a favorite dish and how it tastes, thus integrating sight and taste or smell and taste. Infants are able to do this, to an extent. The skill develops as the child grows and matures.

It is believed that infants less than six months old can categorize objects based on different characteristics, such as shape, size, color, number, density, etc. In conjunction, it is theorized that 12-month-old children can distinguish between types of animals of the same species. For example, a child who grows up with two dogs knows the difference between the dogs.

Language Development:

Children are born with the innate mechanics to learn any language. Generally speaking, children master most levels of spoken language by the age of four or five. Regardless of language or culture, all children appear to transition through the same learning-language stages. One of the first stages of language development is crying. As language capabilities develop, children begin to babble nonsense syllables and phonemes. A **phoneme** is a unit of sound at the beginning stages of language all children babble similar phonemes. Phonemes are shaped and molded as children are exposed to different languages. **Noam Chomsky** was a prominent language psychologist who was the first to see evidence that all babies are born with mechanics for language learning. Children who are exposed to sign language begin to use hand babbling long before using verbal babbling and eventually learns to sign. The neural pathways for kinesthetic language develop before the neural pathways for verbal language.

During the first year of life, children start to narrow phonemes to those of the languages they are exposed to the most, including manual (signed) languages. Words and signs are added rapidly to the point that, by approximately 20 months of age, children have vocabulary of about 20 words. In the subsequent years, a child's vocabulary expands to thousands of words and hundreds of signs. The skill of usage of these words and signs varies with children **overextending** or **underextending.** If a child underextends a word, they may use the word to refer to a family dog and no other dog. On the other hand, if a child overextends a word, they may use the word 'dog' to refer to all four-legged animals. How fast and how well a child learns language is affected by the communication between those who around the child the most. The high-pitched and simplified sounds that babies produce, along with the sounds and phonemes which mothers produce in response are complex communications. These communications are a form of conservation of questions and commands.

Social and Emotional Development:

From the beginning, children begin to develop socially and emotionally. It is clearly evident that infants have distinct feelings towards different people, objects, and experiences. Children show clear attachment toward a loving primary caregiver. This attachment often leads to separation anxiety and stranger anxiety. Such anxieties peak at different ages for different children, with the average child peaking around twelve to sixteen months and declining after.

Attachment is the infant's tendency to seek interaction with particular individuals in order to feel more secure. **Mary Ainsworth** designed a series of experiments in order to better study infant attachment. She dubbed her study The Strange Situation, which gave insight into the different types of attachment that can form between a child and caregiver.

The Strange Situation:

1. A mother and child were brought into a room with games and toys. The child was allowed to explore and play.
2. After a few moments, a stranger would enter the room and approach the child. The mother would then leave, leaving the child with the stranger.
3. The mother would return shortly thereafter and the stranger would leave.
4. The mother would leave again, after a few moments, and the stranger would return. Then the mother would return, again.

The child was watched through a one-way mirror to see how he or she would react to each of these interactions. The interactions were categorized into three types of attachment:

- **Securely Attached:** These children played with toys and were friendly towards the stranger. When the mother left, the child became distressed, cried, and searched for their mother. Upon the return of the mother, the child would approach her to be comforted. Once comforted by her presence, the child would return to playing with the toys.

- **Insecurely Attached and Avoidant:** These children did not seem to pay special attention to their mother, whether or not shew as in the room. If the child was upset, the stranger was able to comfort them. When the mother returned, the child either ignored her or approached her with caution.

- **Insecurely Attached and Resistant:** These children were clingy to their mothers from the start. They did not want to leave her to play with the toys and if she was not readily available, the child grew anxious. When the mother left the room, the child would become inconsolable. Upon her return, the child appeared ambivalent. The child seemed to be confused, wanting to be picked up, but would become angry and fidgety.

- **Social Referencing:** also referred to as 'monkey see, monkey do'. A child will 'read' the reaction of the mother to the stranger. If the mother was nonplussed by the stranger, the child tended to react in a similar manner. If the mother was upset by something, the child would become upset.

The Strange Situation determined that babies become attached by one year of age and the most influential factor to the attachment of the child is the parental reaction to the child. If the parent was responsive to the child's needs, the child tended to become securely attached. Children whose parents were unresponsive or insensitive tended to be insecurely attached.

Awareness:

During late infancy, a child will begin to recognize themselves as a distinct individual. When placed in front a mirror, a young baby tends to not recognize themselves in the reflection. A child of approximately fifteen months responds and plays with their reflection. By the age of two, most children point to themselves when asked "where is (child's name)?"

Personality:

Personality is a unique, but consistent pattern of thoughts, feelings, and behaviors. There are a variety of forces which can affect personality:

- **Genetic factor:** activity level, attention span, adaptability, temperament, and a plethora of other characteristics have been observed since birth, leading to the notion that these characteristics are genetically inherited. **Temperament** is referred to as the consistent dispositions which reflect personal responses to people and things. Being easily distracted, comforted, or active is part of one's temperament.

Identical twins score higher than fraternal twins or siblings on correlational studies in regards to temperament.

- **Three major temperaments:** Three defining temperaments include extroverted, placid, and shy. These temperaments indicate a level of sociability and both extroversion and shyness have been thoroughly studied. **Jerome Kagan** was a psychologist who researched the notion that shyness is exhibited in the first few months of life. During the first few months of life, inhibition towards new objects or people adds to individual shyness. Temperament has been shown to be consistent throughout life. There are three influential theories that attempt to answer how personality originates:
    - **Learning Theory:**
        - Personality is shaped by reinforcements and punishments by parents
            - Example: If a child is positively reinforced for smiling, the child will be more likely to develop a happy disposition
        - This theory blames parents for a poorly adjusted child.
        - Personality is LEARNED from parents
    - **Psychoanalytic Theory:**
        - Personality is formed during the first four years of life.
        - Freud postulated the **Four Stages of Psychoanalytic Development**, with two of those stages being relevant to the Psychoanalytic Theory:
            - 1. Oral Stage: when the most discovery happens with the mouth and weaning is the most important task
            - 2. Anal Stage: potty training is the most important task to accomplish
                - Freud believed children who failed to accomplish these tasks would become fixated on the stage in which they failed and would incur personality problems. His arguments were widely scrutinized.

- **Psychosocial Theory:**
  - **Erik Erikson** proposed the notion that development, inclusive of personality, occurs through various stages of developmental tasks or crisis. During infancy, there are two developmental stages:
    - **Trust versus Mistrust:** Occurs from birth until approximately one year of age, when infants learn if they can trust the world. If an infant's needs are met, they learn to trust.
    - **Autonomy versus Shame and Doubt:** Beginning at approximately two years of age and lasting for approximately one year, children explore their desires to become more independent. If toddlers are allowed to explore, they learn to become autonomous; however, if children are punished for their explorations, they will doubt their ability for independence.

Non-Parental Daycare:

Another crucial aspect of understanding the psychology of toddlers is to understand where they spend their days. Recent research has shown that quality daycares do not have a detrimental outcome on the development of a child. There has been some research to suggest that the social skills learned in daycare facilities are invaluable. Generally speaking, it appears that children who experience non-parental daycare are often more well-adjusted than their non-daycare attending counterparts. A quality daycare has a low caretaker to child ratio, high levels of sensorimotor involvement, and high levels of health and safety.

Chapter 4: Review Questions

1. What reflex occurs when a child's feet are stroked?
    a. Moro reflex
    b. Stepping reflex
    c. Babinski reflex
    d. Rooting reflex

2. Which mental model helps infants to learn about their environment?
    a. Reversal
    b. Schema
    c. Object Permanence
    d. Assimilation

3. To what, does the term 'marasmus' refer to?
    a. Severe micronutrient malnutrition
    b. Severe macronutrient malnutrition
    c. Severe protein Malnutrition
    d. Severe calcium deficiency

4. What did Mary Ainsworth wish to explore with her experiments?
    a. Attachment types
    b. Personality types
    c. Learning types
    d. Daycare qualities

5. According to Erikson, what are the two stages of development encountered during infancy?
    a. Integrity versus Despair
    b. Autonomy versus Shame and Doubt
    c. Initiative versus Guilt
    d. Trust versus Mistrust

6. A child pushes a toy off a table but does not start to look for it. What perceptual ability has the child not yet developed?
    a. Reversal
    b. Assimilation
    c. Object permanence
    d. Attachment

7. Noam Chomsky is regarded for his research into:
    a. Language acquisition
    b. Reflex development
    c. Attachment
    d. Nutritional deficiencies

8. When hearing a familiar voice, it is easy to imagine how the person appears. This is an example of using?
    a. Intermodal perception
    b. Accommodation
    c. Reversal
    d. Cross-modal perception

9. Attachment bonds are most important for feelings of:
    a. Affection
    b. Security
    c. Self-esteem
    d. Belongingness

10. If an infant uses the term 'bear' for one specific bear and refuses to call any of the others bear by their name, what is the infant displaying?
    a. Babbling
    b. Overextending
    c. Assimilating
    d. Underextending

Chapter 4 Answers:

1. C
2. B
3. B
4. A
5. D
6. C
7. A
8. D
9. B
10. D

Chapter 5: Early Childhood

Overview:

During this chapter, there will be an exploration of the physical, cognitive, and social development which occurs during early childhood. This chapter moves beyond infancy to the next few years of life. In addition, conflicts which arise during this stage will be discussed.

Objectives:

By the end of this chapter, you should be able to recognize, understand, and explain:

- The stages of physical development of a child.
- The stages of social and emotional development of childhood.
- Piaget's Preoperational Stage of Development and Vygotsky's Zone of Proximal Development
- Erikson's and Freud's stages of development during early childhood
- Baumrind's parenting Styles
- Different types of play
- Influences of daycare, divorce, and mass media maltreatment on early childhood development

Physical Development:

During early childhood, children grow rapidly and start to lose the extra baby fat from infancy. Proper nutrition is the easiest factor of physical development that can be controlled during childhood. In the USA, children face the problem of obesity more than they face malnutrition. The main nutritional concern in developed countries is **iron deficiency anemia**. There are many theories that attempt to explain why children surfer any deficiencies in developed countries. Such theories include: children being picky eaters, lack of parental education, age of parents, and socioeconomic disparities of parents.

The brain is the fastest growing part of the body. However, it does not grow by cellular division as much as it does by forming more neural pathways. The more the brain is used and actively engaged, the more it grows; this notion is called 'use it or lose it'. Every time an action or behavior is repeated, the connection between the neurons used to complete the action become stronger. As connections become stronger, a child becomes more coordinated and will have quicker reaction times. The less a connection is used, the weaker it becomes. Weak neural connections can lead to a lack of coordination and slower reflex times.

Increased coordination leads to an increase in control of gross motor skills. Gross motor skills are engaged during certain activities, such as running, jumping, and other large body movements. Fine motor skills take longer to improve as young children (generally speaking) have not developed the muscular control, the patience, or the judgment necessary to utilize these skills. Children in the years after infancy are active and spend much of their time exploring their surrounding environment. The number one cause of mortality of young children is accidental death related to drowning, choking, and poisoning. There are different risk factors that increase the risk for accidental death, suxh as gender, socioeconomic status (SES), and parental involvement. Children in lower SES were found to be three times more likely to die from an accidental death than their counterparts in other SES categories.

Cognitive Development:

Children of preschool age tend to be **egocentric**, meaning that their view of the world is from their own perspective and no one else's. Despite being egocentric, preschoolers are not necessarily selfish or self-centered. By the end of early childhood, children begin to understand how others feel and may begin to exhibit empathy. Children may begin to exhibit empathy before this stage, which is dependent on the parental involvement and surrounding environments. A child's intellectual and language skills develop in conjunction with increased memory capabilities.

A child's memory during this stage is not mature enough to handle complex memories or the retrieval of such memories. Children rely on **scripts**, or visual outlines, of common occurrences in their lives. Scripts help children to remember the verbal and speech memories which coincide with familiar visual events. Generally speaking, children do not remember events well before the age of three or four years. Before this age, children have difficulty encoding and retrieving information, which may contribute to the inability to recall memories.

Based on the stages outlined by Jean Piaget, a child in this age range is in the **preoperational stage.** The preoperational stage lasts until approximately age six. During this stage, a child may not be able to perform complex mental operations, but their language usage improves. Preoperational implies that a child is moving towards performing more complex 'operations.' The significant linguistic milestone of the preoperational stage is the ability to use symbols to communicate, referred to as **semiotic function**. A child may assume that if two objects share a quality, the two objects are identical. This is referred to as **transductive reasoning**. For example, a child may call all four-legged animals 'dogs', even if they are not. Another preoperational characteristic is **centration**. Centration is the tendency to have 'tunnel vision', which means to only focus on one object or activity at a time and to be intensely attracted to it.

Piaget studied children's ability to reason and use logic. The principles of those studied are:

- **Conservation:** The understanding that the amount or number is unaffected by the object's shape or placement.
    - **Classic conservation experiment:** A child is presented with two short, wide glasses, each with the same volume of liquid. The child is then asked to pour the contents of one of the short glasses into a tall, slim glass. Due to the inability to demonstrate conservation, the child may assert that the tall glass has more liquid in it than the short glass because the level of liquid is higher.
- **Irreversibility:** The inability of the child to understand that actions, when performed, can be undone to return to the original state.
    - **Classic irreversibility experiment:** a child's favorite toy is covered with a blanket. The child may not understand the toy is still there, just under the blanket, due to the inability to process irreversibility.

Language and Grammar:

Lev Vygotsky refined the cognitive development work of Piaget, focusing more on language development. Vygotsky believed the people in a child's life were influential for developing the child's world and their language capabilities. He believed there were a few vital components for language development.

- **Private speech:**
    - Talking to oneself
    - Represents externalized thought, which leads to communication
    - Eventually becomes inaudible and turns into verbal thought
- **Zone of Proximal Development (ZPD):**
    - Difference between what a child can do independently and what the child needs help with
    - Children learn faster by pushing the boundaries of the ZPD
    - Typically children with wider zones are better able to learn

Vygotsky postulated that children begin to utilize grammar and language rules during early childhood. Children frequently overgeneralize these rules which leads to overextension. A common example of overgeneralization is pluralizing nouns by adding an 's' to the end of all nouns. 'Dog' becomes 'dogs' and to a child who is overextending, 'tooth' becomes 'tooths.'

Language components of psychological importance are:
1. Phonemes: sounds
2. Morphemes: basic units of the meaning of words
3. Syntax: grammar of language
4. Semantics: study of word choice
5. Pragmatics: language variation in societal context

What children learn in schools influences what they learn about language. School and proper education have become increasingly important at early ages. Through research and studies, it has been determined the earlier a child begins their education, the greater their achievements will be in later academic pursuits. Significant components of quality preschool education are: low student-teacher ratio, well-trained staff, and a curriculum that focuses on using creative play to promote cognitive development.

Social and Emotional Development:
Children in the stage of early childhood are generally allowed to explore their world and environment. This freedom allows children to grow in self-confidence and social skills. As children age, they become more aware of themselves as individuals. A child may start to describe themselves physically and emotionally.

According to **Erik Erikson**, children of this age are in the **Initiative versus Guilt Stage,** which lasts until approximately age five. Children play, interact with others, and participate in conversations and activities throughout their days. Due to the variety of activities and environments which surround a child, children develop initiative. If children are not allowed to explore, they will inevitably have insecurities about accomplishing tasks independently and guilt when doing so.

Learning Theories:
Unlike psychoanalysts, learning theorists emphasized the notion that gender roles are learned and modeled inside and outside of the home. Parents tend to reward behavior they deem as gender-appropriate. In addition, parents tend to be critical of gender behavior. The **Baby X Experiments** showed that when adults believed a child was a girl, they encouraged passive play and commented

more about beauty. When the *same* child was portrayed as a boy, the adults emphasized strength, size, and active play. Media influences direct orientation in children. Parents control what media influences themselves and their children.

Parent-Child Relationships:

Regardless of the style of parenting, different styles have been greatly shown to affect children's behaviors. **Diana Baumrind** observed children in nursery schools and interviewed their parents at home. Through her observations, she discovered four differing qualities between parenting styles. The qualities were parental warmth, ability to control the child's actions, quantity/quality of communication between parent and children, and the parental expectation for age-appropriate behavior in their children. There are three distinctive styles of parenting which have been determined from the interviews conducted by Baumrind:

1. **Authoritarian parents:**
    a. Strict rules and rely on punishment to enforce the rules
    b. Standards are high and communication is usually low
    c. Warmth towards the child is low
    d. Do not explain reasons for rules

Children of these parents tend to be obedient without the opportunity to be truly independent.

2. **Permissive parents:**
    a. Effectively opposite of authoritarian parents
    b. Rarely set rules and behavior seldom punished
    c. Expectations are low and communication is high
    d. Warmth is high

Children of these parents may have low self-confidence and demonstrate poor behavior in social situations.

3. **Authoritative Parents:**
    a. Set limits and provide guidance
    b. High expectations and high communication
    c. High levels of warmth
    d. Parents are willing to compromise and listen to their children
    e. Children of these parents are happy, well-adjusted, generous, and independent.

Other styles of parenting have been studied and include: democratic-indulgent and rejecting-neglecting styles. Both of these styles have low expectations or demands and punishment is not relied upon as a method of control. These styles differ in warmth: democratic-indulgent parents are warm and responsive to their children, while rejecting-neglecting parents are cold and disengaged.

Sibling Relationships and Birth Order:

Relationships between siblings are complicated and differ from parent-child and peer relationships. Sibling relationships are the longest relationships of a child's life and they tend to be intense relationships. Sibling rivalry often begins during the preschool years because children begin to compete for parental attention.

Birth order has been researched intensely and such research has provided many conclusions. Only children tend to be verbal earlier, more creative, and struggle in the social relationships. When only children are exposed to social experiences, they develop the social skills other children demonstrate. The eldest children tend to achieve more in traditional fields, while middle and younger children achieve more in creative or social fields. Of course, there are exceptions to every rule or generality. The temperament and personality of a child are more influential factors of future achievement than birth order.

Play Behaviors:

Preschool and kindergarten age children are active people. Children in this age range play with most children their age, but start to show favoritism to one gender of peers. Many types of 'play behavior' can be observed in children of this age range:

- **Unoccupied behavior:** the child does not actively play, but stands and contemplates playing
- **Solitary play:** children play by themselves with toys that are different than the toys near their person
- **Onlooker behavior:** a child may watch others play, but will not play with them.
- **Parallel play:** children play next to (parallel) other children using similar toys
- **Associated play:** children play together in a disorganized manner
- **Cooperative Play:** children play together in an organized manner

The aforementioned types of play can be categorized and classified by:

1. **Functional play:** simple, repetitive motions with or without toys
2. **Constructive play:** using objects to construct something

3. **Dramatic play:** using imaginary situations and games with rules

The Media:
The media, particularly television, has a considerable effect on society. It is estimated that by age sixteen, the average child spends more time in front of a television than in a classroom. The average US household has at least one TV, which is on for approximately seven hours per day. The television is a tool which can harm or benefit due to its ability to affect the ideas and behaviors of individuals.

One of the most pressing concerns with the influence of media is violence. Studies have looked into the effects of viewing violence directly and indirectly (in person or via media, respectively). One study involved two groups of children: one of which viewed violent cartoons, while the other watched nonviolent cartoons. After the study, the children who viewed the violent cartoons were more aggressive than their peers who viewed nonviolent cartoons. The general fear of introducing gratuitous violence to children is that they will become desensitized to it. Studies have shown that if children become desensitized to violence, they may start to believe it is acceptable to act in violent ways.

Childhood Fears:
Generally speaking, **fear** is an anxious response to objects or stimuli. Some fears are 'healthy' because they serve for purposes of self-preservation (e.g. having a fear of fire). Some children have fears which lead to a child being withdrawn, clingy, or anxious. Fear of tangible objects or stimuli (e.g. dogs or moving vehicles) tends to decrease during early childhood, while fear of intangible objects or anticipated events, such as accidents, tends to increase. Childhood fears are often unpredictable and differ from one child to the next. It has been shown that intelligence may influence the likelihood that a child will develop a fear to an object or entity. The number of fears expressed in children from the age of two to five was positively correlated to IQ levels. Female children are more likely to exhibit fearful behaviors than males. Children may also acquire fears from observing their parents, specifically their mothers. If a mother shows fear towards large dogs, a child may pick up on that fear and acquire the fear of large dogs, even if they have had no frightful experience related to dogs.

Concerns which may arise during Early Childhood:
There are significant events which may arise during early childhood and affect development:
1. **Child Maltreatment:**

a. There are an estimated one million cases of child maltreatment yearly in the USA
   b. Maltreatment includes physical, emotional, and sexual abuse as well as physical and emotional neglect
   c. In the USA, child maltreatment rates are higher than other countries for a variety of reasons:
      i. Families of lower SES are shunned and not afforded as many opportunities as families of higher SES.
      ii. There is less social support for parents and a lack of emphasis on what is best for a child. Also, due to lack of close family ties (when compared to many other countries), there is less family support.
      iii. Lack of parental education, as to what to expect from children and how to teach them.
   d. Inflexibility in routine can lead to abuse and neglect
   e. Fewer than ten percent of parents show pathology

Consequences of Maltreatment: Learning difficulties, poor self-esteem, continuing the cycle, and emotional control, to name a few.

Prevention is the most important goal to lower cases of maltreatment. Prevention mechanisms can include: parental education, better jobs, and societal change to support parents.

2. **Daycare:**
   a. It was previously thought that daycare did not influence development.
   b. Now, it has been shown that children who attend a quality preschool are higher academic achievers and have a decreased likelihood of repeating grades.
   c. Preschoolers have been shown to improve social skills, but were shown to be more aggressive and less polite.

3. **Divorce:**
   a. The USA has the highest divorce rate in the world.
   b. Divorce always has negative effects on the children due to the disruption and turmoil it causes.
   c. Children often show signs of emotional pain and stress for the first few years after the divorce.

d. The duration of effects on children after divorce have been studied in longitudinal studies. These studies have shown most children do adjust at a certain point. Effects have been shown to extend into adulthood.
e. The most influential factor for children to be able to cope is the stability of home life. More stability equals better coping skills.

Chapter 5: Review Questions

1. Understanding the amount of liquid in a glass is unaffected by the shape of the glass is:
    a. Overextension
    b. Classification
    c. Conservation
    d. Reversibility

2. The range of potential development is:
    a. Object permanence
    b. Zone of Proximal Development
    c. Classification
    d. Intelligence

3. Applying grammatical rules broadly is:
    a. Division
    b. Differentiation
    c. Overextension
    d. Variability

4. Pattern of play vary in relation to:
    a. Age
    b. Gender
    c. Social class
    d. All of the above

5. According to Erikson, in what direction does parental focus shift as their child matures from infancy to adulthood?
    a. Control to nurture
    b. Love to discipline
    c. Spouse to child
    d. Nurturance to control

6. Which of the following is not a characteristic of the preoperational stage?
    a. Centration
    b. Magical thinking
    c. Empathy
    d. Lack of conservation

7. In which of Erikson's stages does the child begin to identify and pursue goals?
    a. Identity versus Role Confusion
    b. Initiative versus Guilt
    c. Industry verses Inferiority
    d. Autonomy versus Shame and Doubt

8. Watching violence in the media has been shown to cause:
    a. People to commit suicide
    b. An increase in divorce
    c. Desensitization to real violence
    d. Decrease in peer relationships

9. Children who lack self-confidence and do not exhibit many positive behaviors probably have:
    a. Permissive parents
    b. Authoritarian parents
    c. Authoritative parents
    d. Passive parents

10. Early childhood corresponds to which of Freud's stages?
    a. Anal
    b. Phallic
    c. Oral
    d. Genital

Chapter 5 Answers:

1. C
2. B
3. C
4. D
5. D
6. C
7. B
8. C
9. A
10. B

Life Span Developmental Psychology

Chapter 6: Middle Childhood

Overview:

This chapter will delve into the physical, cognitive, social development, and concerns which arise during middle childhood. While the chapters may seem to correlate together in topics, readers should focus on the particulars of the various stages. As a child ages, their growth and development change drastically.

Objectives:

By the end of this chapter, you should be able to recognize, understand, and explain:

- The stages of physical development in the 'school years'
- Piaget's Concrete Operational Stage of Development, along with key principles of logical operations
- Information Processing Theory and metacognition, learning disabilities, and theories of intelligence
- Social cognition, self-esteem, and how peer and family relationships influence social development

Physical Development:

Compared to infancy, Growth during middle childhood slows down. Generally, growth occurs without complications. Children grow taller and slimmer, muscles become stronger, and long capacity increases. Slower growth allows children to become more coordinated and further develop fine motor skills. Children begin to play team sports and exercise more rigorously. Exercise during this stage is crucial. Proper exercise teaches a child to exercise during their life and is the largest deterrent of suffering from obesity. In recent years, children have spent more time indoors for sedentary activities like watching TV or playing video games, which lead to more and more children being diagnosed as obese. In addition to the medical issues which arise from obesity (diabetes and hypertension), psychological problems may occur. Children who suffer from obesity may be bullied and experience depression and low self-esteem. Increasing awareness about the problem and its causes will help prevent problems in the future.

Life Span Developmental Psychology

Cognitive Development:

As a child matures, increased myelination and synapses help a child to improve and refine their behaviors. The increase of myelination and synapses leads to an increase in **automaticity** (automatic behavior), impulse control, and selective attention. **Selective attention** is the ability to concentrate on relevant information, such as a lecture, while ignoring outside distractions. Children learn to plan and problem solve effectively. In addition, children begin to recognize their personal skills and weaknesses. **Metacognition** is the ability to 'think about thinking' or to think about a task and decide how best to accomplish the task. Metacognition develops and matures as a child moves through the middle childhood stage.

Memory continues to improve during this stage of development. Increased memory is helpful as a child enters higher grade levels and must be able to recall more and more information. Storage strategies and retrieval stages help a child to improve their memories.

- **Rehearsal:** repeating information to make sure it is remembered
- **Reorganization:** regrouping information so it is easily remembered

According to Piaget, children are not in the concrete operational stage. The significant characteristics are:

- **Conservation**
- **Reversibility**
- **Classification:** combining objects into categories (toys, food, animals)
- **Seriation:** making an orderly arrangement (large to small)
- **Compensation:** the principle which changes in one dimension can be offset by changes in another dimension

Language:

During middle childhood, communication skills of a child increase and multiply. School aged children increase vocabulary and grammar skills while becoming more logical and analytical. Many schools encourage and push children to learn a second language due to **bilingualism** being shown to improve cognitive development. A younger child's brain plasticity (ability to learn) enables them to learn a second language easily and a variety of concepts.

Intelligence:

As children progress through school, achievement tests are administered to measure how much a child has learned of a particular subject. Aptitude tests are designed to measure cognitive potential and are used to predict academic success or to diagnose learning disabilities. The most common aptitude test is the General Intelligence Test, or IQ Test. **IQ** stands for intelligence quotient and is defined as the mental age divided by the chronological (actual) age. The most frequently used IQ tests are the Stanford-Binet and the Wechsler. Each test measures general knowledge, reasoning ability, memory, math, vocabulary, and spatial perception. There are specialized tests for different age children, even for as young as preschool-aged children. IQ tests need to be used with caution because they are only useful when comparing the results to other children of the same age who took the same test.

One of the largest issues with traditional aptitude and achievement tests are they only measure one kind of intelligence. Robert Sternberg purported three types of intelligence including academic, creative, and practical.

- **Academic intelligence:** measured by IQ tests and achievement tests
- **Creative intelligence:** measured by imaginative pursuits
- **Practical intelligence:** measured by everyday interactions and actions

Howard Gardner believed there are more types of intelligence which include: linguistic, logical-mathematical, musical, spatial, body-kinesthetic, interpersonal, intrapersonal, naturalistic, and philosophical. **Daniel Goleman** supports the idea of **emotional intelligence**, self-control, and the communication of feelings.

Children with Special Needs:

Most special needs, learning disabilities, and emotional handicaps are diagnosed during middle childhood.

1. **Autism**
    a. Named in 1941 by A.D. Kanner
    b. Main symptoms: extreme Isolation and obsessive insistence on routine preservation
    c. Other characteristics: low level of family history
    d. Autistic children tend to avoid overstimulation and dislike changes in their routines
    e. Perform repetitive behaviors such as rocking or spinning to comfort themselves
    f. One theory says that children with Autism are naturally overly stimulated and, as such, they are often prescribed sedative medications

2. **Learning disabilities**
    a. Children with learning disabilities (LDs) have difficulty in mastering one or more basic skills
    b. Difficulties are not generally due to mental retardation or physical handicaps such as deafness
    c. Dyslexia, a reading difficulty, is the most common learning disability
    d. Dyscalculia, a math difficulty, is another common learning disability
    e. Previously, children with LDs were segregated from their peers at school
    f. If possible, children with LDs are mainstreamed into regular education classrooms
    g. The best compromise in the debate of inclusion and exclusion of children with learning disabilities in regular education classrooms is inclusion with an aide into a general education classroom.

3. **Hyperactivity**
    a. Characteristics: Over activity, impulsiveness, restlessness, distractibility, and short attention spans
    b. Usually diagnosed as **Attention Deficit Hyperactivity Disorder (ADHD)**
    c. Related to ADHD symptoms is **Attention Deficit Disorder (ADD),** however these children lack the hyperactivity
    d. Children with ADD or ADHD tend to have difficulties choosing the appropriate emotional or behavioral response to a stimulus
    e. Potential cause: children are thought to be under stimulated during critical periods of learning and brain formation.
    f. Treatment: medication, environmental changes, and structured time

4. **Gifted and talented students**
    a. Unlike children with learning difficulties or special needs, 'gifted' students do not often receive special treatment in schools.
    b. Many states are beginning to provide assistance to schools for superior students
    c. Gifted students usually have average physical, social, and emotional development, but are cognitively, intellectually, and academically advanced.

d. These students tend to be divergent thinkers who respond in unusual ways to questions or problems, while their peers tend to be convergent thinkers who respond in typical ways.
   e. Occasionally, gifted and talented students are placed in accelerated courses.
   f. More often than not, gifted students are simply given 'enrichment' courses or more challenging work

Social and Emotional Development:

During middle childhood, children explore their environments with more independence. The most critical goal to accomplish is the improvement in social cognition or the increased understanding of people and groups. Below are the two influential theories of social and emotional development.

- **Freud**
    - Psychosexual Development Stage: latency
    - Duration: approximately seven to eleven years of age
    - Children focus on the outside world and acquire the cognitive skills needed for adulthood.

- **Erikson**
    - Psychosocial Development Stage: industry versus inferiority
    - Duration: approximately age six to age eleven
    - Children begin to produce things such as school work, artwork, and more. They begin to feel industrious.
    - If this feeling is encouraged by caregivers, the child will continue to be and feel industrious.

    - If the caregivers dismiss, reject, or even punish a child's industriousness, the child will grow to feel inferior.
    - Inferiority complexes may result during this stage.

Self-esteem continues to develop during middle childhood as children tend to become more introspective. One aspect of the development of self-esteem is that children learn to control their reactions and become more self-regulated. There are many external factors which affect the development of self-esteem, such as SES, country of origin, immigrant status, family dynamics, to name a few. An often underestimated factor which impacts an individual's self-esteem is peers. If children are neglected, teased, or bullied, their self-esteems may decrease.

Family structure can help with self-esteem. The makeup of the family structure does not matter. For example, it does not matter if the parents are single or married, the sexual orientation of the parents, or if there is extended family living in the house. A low conflict, highly supportive home environment plays a very important role in a child's development of self-esteem.

Difficulties of Adjustments:

There are many times of adjustment during middle childhood. These periods of adjustment can be anything from moving, new school years, family differences, etc. Times of adjustment can cause anxieties, frustrations, and even aggressiveness. Aggressive behaviors have been shown to be more prevalent in males than females, especially in regards to physical aggression. Males tend to learn more via observation, than females. Female children tend to mimic emotional manipulation they observe, while male children tend to mimic physical aggression they observe. **Freud** postulated the **Frustration-Aggression Hypothesis**, which states that whenever someone's effort to obtain a goal is blocked, the result is frustration. Frustration may lead to aggression because the desired goal was obstructed. Aggression is cause by frustration and aggression is an innate drive in all people.

Alfred Bandura put forth the notion of **Social Learning Theory**, which differs from behavioral theories in that Social Learning Theory emphasizes the importance of cognitive processes of the learning experience. Based on Social Learning Theory, aggression is learned via observation and the more it is observed, the more the aggression is repeated. Bandura set up the 'Bobo Doll Experiment' which allowed two groups of children to watch videos of other children's interaction with the Bobo doll. Each group of children was allowed to play with the doll after viewing their respective videos. The children, who had viewed the video with violence that went unpunished, exhibited violence and aggression towards the doll. However, the children who had viewed the video where violence was punished were reluctant to be aggressive towards the doll.

Possible Conflicts in Middle Childhood:
1. **Social phobias**
    a. Stem from a fear of leaving home and being away from parents
    b. More common in females than males
    c. Deeper issue is generally separation anxiety from both parents and child

2. **Divorce**
    a. Huge potential for destructive effect, such as hostility between parents
    b. More conflict between parents leads to increased depression and anger in children
    c. Critical to maintain adequate care of the child between homes
    d. Children may benefit from continued contact with both parents
3. **Coping with life**
    a. Coping abilities are related to cognitive abilities
    b. Support is the most important element for coping with life
    c. Children who are forced to cope with a singular stress, or few stresses, are no more likely to have psychological problems than those without stress
    d. Additional stress may cause significant damage
4. **Homelessness**
    a. There are between 50,000-100,000 homeless children every night in the USA and half of these children are school-aged
    b. Homeless children have fewer friends, more fear, and more illness
    c. These children tend to be behind in academic achievement
    d. Clinical depression affects at least thirty percent of these children

Chapter 6: Review Questions

1. What is the educational approach which places special needs children in a general classroom?
    a. Exclusion
    b. Mainstreaming
    c. Resource room utilization
    d. Enrichment

2. Which of the following is a gender schema?
    a. Women wear dresses
    b. Women have more mental disorders than men
    c. Little boys wear blue, little girls wear pink
    d. A and C, but not B

3. Who developed the Theory of Multiple Intelligences?
    a. Gardner
    b. Stern
    c. Simon
    d. Binet

4. A child did not score well on a traditional IQ Test, but understands people well and gets along with many different people. What type of intelligence is he or she exhibiting?
    a. Kinesthetic
    b. Interpersonal
    c. Intrapersonal
    d. Naturalistic

5. The ability to evaluate a cognitive task to determine the best way to accomplish it is?
    a. Concrete Operations
    b. Metacognition
    c. Reversibility
    d. Classification

6. The ability to concentrate on relevant information and to ignore distractions is:
    a. Selective attention
    b. Centration
    c. Formal Operations
    d. Classification

7. Myelination in middle childhood most likely leads to:
    a. Greater short-term memory
    b. Greater long-term memory
    c. Better focus and attention
    d. A and B, but not C

8. Dimension of intelligence which refers to self-understanding is:
    a. Interpersonal
    b. Naturalistic
    c. Philosophical
    d. Intrapersonal

9. The most dramatic shift in middle childhood relationships is characterized by:
    a. Breaking attachments with parents
    b. Developing an interest in the opposite sex
    c. Learning to identify with teachers
    d. Developing same-sex peer groups

10. Childhood obesity is caused by:
    a. Attitudes towards food
    b. Hereditary influences
    c. Lack of exercise
    d. All of the above

Chapter 6 Answers:

1. B
2. D
3. A
4. B
5. B
6. A
7. C
8. D
9. D
10. D

Life Span Developmental Psychology

Chapter 7: Adolescence

Overview:
During this chapter, the physical, cognitive, and social development of adolescence will be explored. In addition, conflicts and concerns which may arise during this time are discussed. This framework provides another layer for a strong foundation in understanding development across the lifespan.

Objectives:
By the end of this chapter, you should be able to recognize, understand, and explain:

- Stages of physical development in adolescence
- Piaget's Formal Operational Stage of Development along with principles of adolescent egocentrism proposed by **Elkind**
- Marcia's research about identity statuses and characteristics
- Influence of family, peers, and vocations of adolescents

Physical Development:
Adolescence is marked by the onset of a period of physical growth, puberty, , and sexual maturation. Most adolescents begin puberty between eight and fourteen years old. Females generally begin puberty two years earlier than boys. Females reach menarche between the ages of nine and sixteen, but genetics play a role in the age of menarche. Sisters typically experience their first menstrual periods an average of thirteen months apart. Identical twins reach menarche approximately 2.8 months apart.

Puberty is triggered by hormonal changes. These hormonal changes can be triggered by the environment. Due to environmental changes, specifically hormones and antibiotics, puberty is beginning earlier. The hormonal changes lead to physical changes in both males and females, leading to the appearance of secondary sex characteristics.

- **Males**: growth of testes, penis, pubic hair, first ejaculation, voice changes, development of facial hair, and growth spurts
- **Females**: breast growth, pubic hair, first menstrual period (menarche), widening of the hips, and growth spurts.

A **growth spurt** is characterized by a sudden and rapid growth of the entire body. The extremities grow first, then the torso and the rest of the body. Internal organs increase in size and functional capacity. During the average adolescent growth spurt, females grow approximately 3.5 inches and males grow approximately 4 inches.

Hormones of Puberty:
Due to the wide range of ages during when puberty may occur, there are 'early bloomers' and 'late bloomers.' Children who are either early or late bloomers are often bullied and ostracized. Such teasing may lead to a poor body image, an increased risk of eating disorders, or other psychiatric problems. The main hormones are:

- **Testosterone:** more prevalent in males. Helps to produce sperm and is associated with sex drive, aggression, and muscle development
- **Estrogen:** more prevalent in females. Helps to produce eggs and is associated with libido, sexual interest, reproductive cycle, and muscle development

Health and Hazards of Adolescence:
Adolescence is a healthy period, as the risk of childhood diseases is virtually gone and the diseases of old age do not typically occur during this age range. The main concerns of poor health and hazards are:

- **Nutrition**
    - Extra vitamins and minerals are needed due to intense growth spurts
    - Increased caloric need
    - Few American adolescents consume enough fruits and vegetables
    - Iron deficiency is common, especially in females
- **Risky behavior**
    - Adolescents tend to engage in risky behavior, more so than any other age group
    - Behaviors serve to separate from parents and gain social status. Adolescents learning to stand alone
    - Behaviors include: car accidents, sexual promiscuity, drug/alcohol abuse, and disregard for parental direction
- **Drug use**
    - The majority of teenagers have tried alcohol or drugs before graduating high school

- o Tobacco, alcohol, and marijuana are typically thought of as 'gateway' drugs to more serious drugs
- o Risk of addiction increases as the age of first drug use/drink decreases
- **Sexual Abuse**
  - o Children between ages seven and thirteen are at the greatest risk for sexual abuse
  - o Sexual abuse is any sexual activity, or activity which can be interpreted as sexual, without consent from all persons involved
  - o Legal age of consent is set by state law, and is usually between fourteen and sixteen years of age
  - o Sexual abuse is still abuse if consent is not given or revoked, regardless of legal age of consent
  - o Sexual activity with someone younger than the legal age of consent, even if consent is given, is considered abuse
  - o Sexual abusers are typically men that the child knows Females are abused more often than males
  - o Sexual abuse and abuse in general, occur across all races, genders, SES, and ethnicities.

Adolescent Cognition:

Cognitive development continues throughout the adolescent period:

- Selective attention improves
- Memory improves
- Metacognition (thinking about thinking) improves

According to **Piaget**, adolescents fall into the **Formal Operational Thought** category. This stage is the final stage in Piaget's cognitive developmental timeline. Formal Operational Thought is characterized by the ability to think hypothetically, logically, and abstractly. These skills start to become evident by age twelve. Adolescents have the ability to think about the future in a symbolic manner. Their ability to complete tasks with abstract ideals is the significant characterization of this stage. Adolescents can also perform hypothetico-deductive reasoning to consider the many solutions to a single problem, weight options, and make an informed decision.

Adolescent egocentrism leads an individual to focus on themselves, often believing they are more important or more skilled than others. An adolescent spends considerable time hypothesizing the opinions of others and using these hypotheses as facts. Psychologist **David Elkind** hypothesized that adolescents exhibit such behaviors due to the inability to differentiate between the unique and the universal. An extension of adolescent egocentrism is the **Invincibility Fallacy**, in which adolescents believe the dangers connected to high risk behaviors cannot befall them. The personal fable is the idea that adolescents believe they are heroic, unique, or destined for fame. This notion can lead to an inflated sense of self, but can also be a motivator at times. Adolescents also tend to act as if their lives are interesting to everyone and that the "world is a stage." They feel as though the rest of the world is an **imaginary audience**, who is as concerned with the life of the adolescent as much as the adolescent.

Adolescent Sexual Activity:

Adolescents are becoming sexually active at younger ages across the globe than in previous years. Because of younger ages of activity and lack of proper education, adolescents are at a higher risk for contracting sexually transmitted infections (STI) or diseases (STD). These infection and disease include, but are not limited to: syphilis, gonorrhea, herpes, chlamydia, human papilloma virus, and HIV. In addition to disease and infection risk, adolescents also face the possibility of unwanted pregnancies. In recent years, 80% of teenage mothers remain unmarried and almost all enter the workforce. In comparison, teenage mothers in the 1960s were married before children and stayed home. It is believed one of the main reasons for poor life choices is the lack of good judgment and good examples to follow. Sexual activity is further affected by the notion of the Invincibility Fallacy.

Many schools are steering away from 'abstinence only' and toward teaching choices adolescents have to protect themselves, if they choose to become sexually active. Some say it is difficult to assess the effectiveness of sex education programs due to the wide variety of cultures, language, and sexuality (straight, homosexual, etc.). Despite the variety amongst adolescents, there is a general consensus that teenagers are more open to talking about sex than were previous generations. However, sexuality tends to remain a personal and private matter until the individual decides it is appropriate to share their opinions.

Adolescent Morality:

Lawrence Kohlberg was at the forefront of moral development research. This research used moral dilemmas to classify levels of moral reasoning among children from ages ten to sixteen. In his experiment, he posed the question "Why shouldn't you steal from a store?" After posing the question, he scored each response and then developed three levels and six stages of moral reasoning.

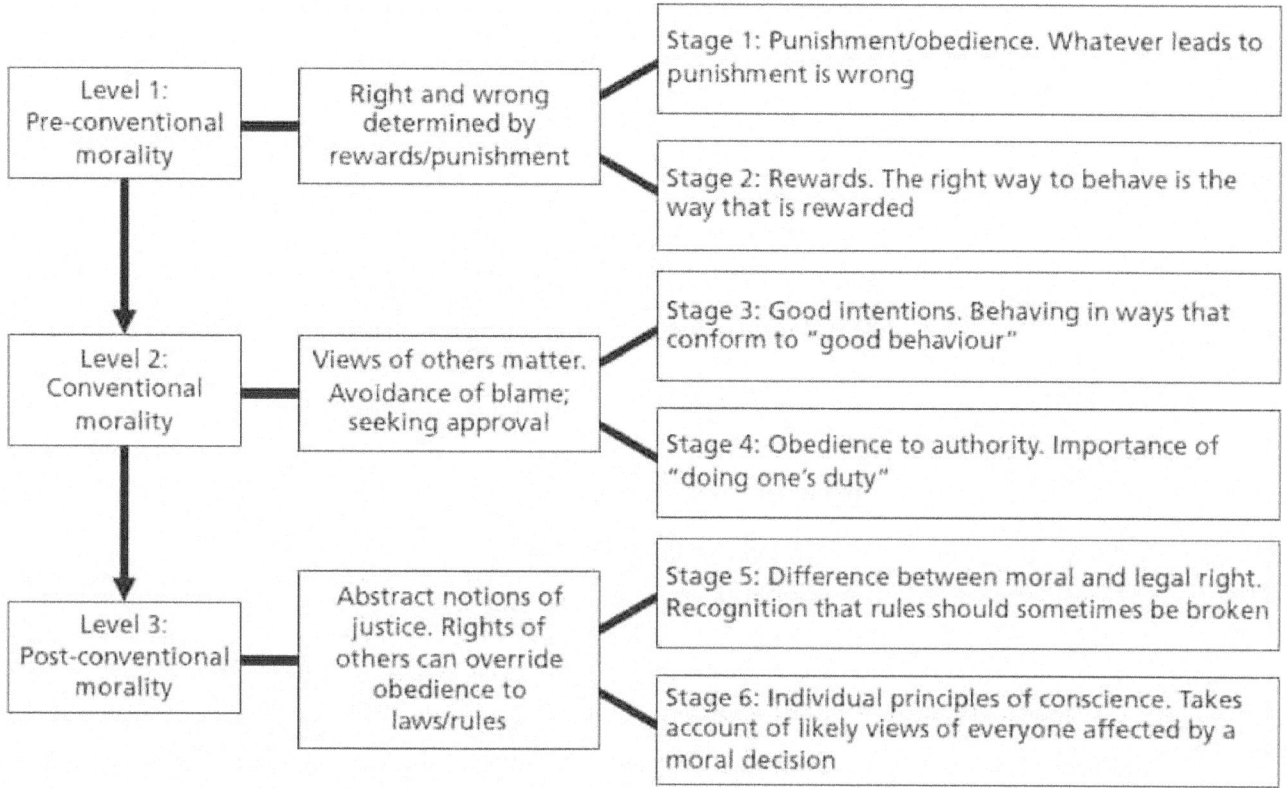

Source: www.integratesociopsychology.net

Kohlberg's theories have been challenged on several occasions. Psychologist **Carol Gilligan** suggested Kohlberg's research was gender biased because Kohlberg only used male adolescents in his experiment. According to Gilligan, females give more moral weight to relationships and do not see moral issues in "black and white." Due to this difference of moral weight, females tend to score low on Kohlberg's test.

Adolescent Psychosocial Development:

According to **Erik Erikson**, an adolescent is in the **Identity versus Role Confusion** stage of development. Due to this conflict, adolescents experience identity crisis and act out of a "false self" which tends to be in opposition to their true self. Between the ages of twelve and eighteen, adolescents attempt to separate from their parents to determine the person they want to become. If adolescents successfully combine their multiple roles, they will achieve a coherent sense of identity.

James Marcia developed four identity statuses:

1. **Identity Achievement**
    a. Individual knows he is unique
    b. Includes sexual, moral, political, and vocational identity
2. **Foreclosure**
    a. Premature identity formation
    b. Individual accepts parental values and goals without consideration to options
3. **Identity Diffusion**
    a. Uncertainty and confusion regarding identity
    b. Leads to apathetic behavior
4. **Moratorium**
    a. Pause in identity formation
    b. Individual explores alternatives
    c. Example: the year before college, college years, temporary job

Another interesting aspect of exploring identity is that of **cultural identity.** Many adolescents strive to explore their cultural or racial identities. Often this endeavor leads a bicultural identity or a blending of personal cultures. Being able to operate and thrive in multiple cultures is associated with higher self-esteem and confidence.

Parenting and Peers:

Parenting styles never cease to affect how a child matures and learns. Adolescents with authoritative parents tend to be more psychologically healthy and undergo positive psychosocial development. In this situation, the adolescent is allowed to be independent while being warmly supported by their parents. Adolescents of authoritative parents display fewer risky behaviors, which differs greatly in their peers who have permissive parents.

Peers are an important source of information and influence for adolescents. In early adolescence, most friendships exist between same-gender individuals. As an individual moves through adolescence, they tend to make friend of the opposite gender. Friendships tend to fall into categories of crowd, clique, and individual.

Life Span Developmental Psychology

- **Crowd**: the most inclusive and least personal. Usually a group of people with mutual interests (e.g. band, drama, debate)
- **Clique**: intimate, interpersonal relationships Clique membership may be a prerequisite for crowd membership
- **Individual**: most intimate and the most exclusive. This may be a prerequisite for clique membership

Vocational Choices:

Choosing a vocation during adolescence has become more difficult in recent years. There are many more choices available and each choice has a specific skill set requirement. While jobs are becoming more specialized, schools are trending to becoming more generalized. This disparity is leading to many individuals being unprepared for the workforce. As time progresses, automatic processes and artificial intelligence do as well. The opportunities for unskilled or semi-skilled laborers are becoming fewer by the day.

Social class is an important role in choosing vocations. Generally speaking, adolescents from higher social classes are more likely to aspire to a professional or business occupation as a career goal, whereas, individuals from a lower SES tend to not have such aspirations and often envision themselves in service or trade occupations. Peer groups may alter their vocational choices. Depending on the environment, support, and influences in an individual's life, the vocational choice may not be typical of their SES.

Concerns and Conflicts of Adolescence:

Below are a few of the main conflicts and concerns which can often arise during adolescence. There are many theories about what causes these events to occur and few ideas for treatment and prevention.

- **School dropouts**
    - Dropouts face immense career problems, as most positions require some sort of education
    - Tend to come from lower SES families
    - Individuals face a higher risk of delinquency, criminal behavior, and drug addiction
- **Juvenile delinquency**

- o Individuals are more likely to be arrested in their 20s than in any other decade of their lives
- o Identifying and aiding adolescents prone to delinquency is important to help prevent future issues; however, it is not the perfect prevention
- o The earlier an individual starts displaying delinquent behavior, the likelihood of them achieving future endeavors decreases

- **Suicide**
    - o Suicidal thoughts are becoming more and more common among adolescents
    - o Worldwide, females are more likely to attempt suicide while males are more likely to complete suicide
    - o Generally speaking, most cases of suicide are preceded by a significant negative event
    - o Some signs and symptoms of suicide:
        - Giving away possessions
        - Withdrawing from friends, family, and school
        - Talking about suicide plans
        - A sudden mood increase because a decision has been made
    - o Recognizing these signs is the best prevention method for suicide.

Chapter 7: Review Questions

1. Puberty is:

    a. Marked by rapid physical growth and changes in reproductive anatomy

    b. Triggered only by the environment

    c. Usually earlier in males and females

    d. Occurring later in life now than in previous years

2. Sexual abuse is:

    a. Any act, of an explicit or implicit sexual nature, which is done or attempted without consent from all parties

    b. Usually in situations where prevention was not attempted

    c. Most commonly committed by males who know the victim

    d. Particular to a social class, gender, or race

3. The ability to postulate a multitude of solutions to a given problem and to choose the most appropriate solution is:

    a. Egocentrism

    b. Classification

    c. Hypothetico-deductive reasoning

    d. Inductive reasoning

4. The egocentric notion of adolescents who assume others are interested in their lives is:

    a. Centration

    b. Formal Operational Thought

    c. Imaginary audience

    d. Personal fable

5. Emphasis on rewards and punishment for unacceptable behavior places an individual in what category of Kohlberg's research?

    a. Post-conventional Morality Level

    b. Pre-conventional Morality Level

    c. Law and Order Stage
    d. Conventional Morality Level

6. Tom is an adolescent who is now questioning his Catholic faith, which has been passed to him through his family. He has begun to explore other types and approaches to religion. What status would Tom be in, according to Marcia?
    a. Diffusion
    b. Moratorium
    c. Foreclosure
    d. Commitment

7. Which parenting style has been shown to help prevent adolescent children from engaging in risky behavior?
    a. Authoritarian
    b. Permissive
    c. Authoritative
    d. Negligent

8. Rachel has always been told she is going to be a doctor, like her parents. Due to this, she has never considered alternate vocational options. What identity status, according to Marcia, would she be in?
    a. Foreclosure
    b. Moratorium
    c. Achieved
    d. Diffusion

9. Adolescents, who are multicultural, and develop a multicultural identity tend to:
    a. Achieve a high social outcome
    b. Have high self-esteem
    c. Have low self-esteem
    d. Both A and B

10. Kohlberg is criticized for:
    a. Only having male participants
    b. Not following ethical procedures
    c. Viewing females separately than men, with regards to moral development
    d. Not considering gender-specific factors in moral reasoning

Chapter 7 Answers:

1. A
2. C
3. C
4. C
5. B
6. B
7. C
8. A
9. D
10. A

Life Span Developmental Psychology

Chapter 8: Early Adulthood

Overview:

This chapter will delve into the physical, cognitive, and social development of early adulthood. During this life stage, conflicts and concerns differ from the previous stages. In addition, key developmental milestones and challenges individuals face and overcome during this age are explored.

Objectives:

By the end of this chapter you should be able to recognize, understand, and explain:

- Stages of physical change during early adulthood
- Sexual reproductive systems and infertility issues
- Post-Formal and dialectal thought process, the influence of education, and the impact of life events on cognitive development
- Concepts of intimacy, friendship, cohabitation, marriage, divorce, and parenthood
- Different theoretical perspectives of early adulthood psychosocial development
- Importance if work including work patterns, workplace diversity, and dual-income families

Physical Development and Changes:

Early adulthood begins at approximately twenty years of age and lasts until approximately forty years of age. Early adulthood is often considered the 'prime of life' because physical performance is at its peak and if regular physical activity is maintained, there are few noticeable signs of aging during this stage. Between the ages of fifteen and thirty, growth ceases, and **senescence** begins. Senescence is a period of physical decline, loss of strength, and loss of efficiency. Despite the variation of the aging process, there is a commonality all individuals share: the human body does not function the same way at forty years of age, as it did at twenty years of age.

By the age of twenty, growth spurts and hormones start to calm down. Height increases begin to cease, while muscle growth and adipose (fat) stores continue to increase. Digestive, respiratory, and reproductive systems are functioning at their optimal level during this age range. Health problems are usually rare. The main function of physicians during this stage is to treat sports injuries and pregnancy. Death is caused by accidents more often than anything else.

During early adulthood, many individuals begin families. Unfortunately, fifteen percent of couples experience **infertility**, or the inability to conceive easily. There are many medical infertility interventions, including in vitro fertilization and artificial insemination by donor, to name a few. There are many causes and influences on infertility, age is one of them. Below are more causes of infertility:

- **Male Infertility**
    - Low sperm count or malformed sperm
    - Age, childhood illness, prescription drug use, cigarette smoking, and stress
- **Female Infertility**
    - Age, childhood illness, prescription drug use, cigarette smoking, and stress
    - Weight: over or under weight contributes to infertility
    - Failure to ovulate (most common cause of infertility)
    - High acidity in the reproductive tract destroys sperm

Concerns and Conflicts of Early Adulthood:

The most pressing concerns of health and wellness which early adulthood individuals face include drug abuse, destructive dieting, and eating disorders in addition to accidents and depression.

- **Drug Abuse**
    - Adolescents and early adults are the heaviest drug users
    - Drug Use: ingesting any drug, regardless of amount or frequency
    - Drug Abuse: using a drug in a manner which is physically detrimental
    - Drug Addiction: a condition of drug dependence
- **Dangerous Dieting**
    - Repetitive dieting can be unhealthy
    - Almost all 'crash' diets involve nutritional imbalance, energy loss, and vulnerability to disease
    - Results in an individual being dangerously underweight and in serious risk of major health problems.
- **Eating Disorders**
    - Anorexia: restricted caloric intake to the point of emaciation or starvation
    - Bulimia: compulsive binge eating followed by purging through vomiting or laxative use

- Regression Theory: **Freud** suggests anorexia is a subconscious manifestation against maturation
- Cultural Image Theory: says media suggest unrealistic weight expectations for the general population to emulate
- Control Theory: states that due to a lack of control in life, an individual may eat excessively.
- Typically, younger individuals are more often affected and those from higher SES tend to be diagnosed more than those from lower SES.

- **Death**
  - Is not particular to a race, gender, or culture
  - Includes accidents, homicides, or suicides
  - Some studies suggest that males are more likely to die during early adulthood than females.

Cognitive Development in Early Adulthood:

During early adulthood, physical changes slowly decelerate, while cognitive changes increase. Stores of knowledge, speed of cognition, information processing efficiency, and thought content all accelerate. Individuals learn to think and behave in more practical, integrative, and resourceful ways.

Post-Formal Thought is less abstract than Formal Thought. During the early adulthood years, an individual uses reasoning which helps them to better focus on solving problems in 'real life.' Post-Formal Thought dictates that a person transitions from the clear decisions (black and white approach) of Formal Thought, to recognizing the areas of grey when facing problems.

The three main characteristics of Post-Formal Thought are:

1. **Relativism:** Refers to the understanding that one's personal perspective is only one of the many potentially valid views of reality. Knowledge is not fixed or absolute.
2. **Acceptance of contradiction:** Implies the understanding that reality embraces inconsistencies. A person can love someone and be angry with that person at the same time.
3. **Integration:** Integration is a deep and refined thought process. An individual gains the capacity to integrate and synthesize conflicting ideas or views into a more coherent whole. Integration advances an individual far beyond earlier stages, when an individual felt as if they had to choose between sides.

Dialectal thought is the ability to understand the pros and cons and the plethora of possibilities of a given situation. In addition, dialectal thought involves continual thought integration, formation of a belief (or a thesis), formation of an opposing belief (antithesis), and creative **synthesis** to join all components of a situation to form a conclusion.

It is believed that a component of cognitive growth in early adulthood is due to the enrollment in **higher education** (post-high school education). Gender ratios have flipped and in recent years, approximately fifty-five percent of college students are female. There has been an increase in the percentages of Hispanic, Asiatic, African-American, and other races and ethnicities of students enrolling in higher educational institutions. Approximately twenty percent of citizens and residents of the USA hold at least a bachelor's degree. Higher education does more than educate via academic material; Generally speaking, it encourages flexible thinking, tolerance, and allows individuals to feel a sense of control over their lives. Regardless of the type and form of higher education, certain skills increase and develop, such as verbal, math, formal reasoning, and critical thinking.

Beyond the scope of higher education, certain **life events** help an individual to mature cognitively. Parenthood is an event which sparks maturity in most individuals. Other life events, such as religious experiences, a new job, or a new relationship, encourage maturation. No matter the life event, the commonality is when the event occurs; the individual is forced to view their life from a new perspective, which tends to promote maturation.

Psychosocial Development in Early Adulthood:

There are two foundational themes which drive adult development, the need to feel connected to other human beings and to feel independent in the individual's ability to support themselves and others. **Maslow** suggested the need to belong and feel love is the primary force behind development. **Freud** purported that a healthy adult was one who could love and work and the ability to do so was the driving force behind development.

Erikson believed a young adult is typically in the **Intimacy versus Isolation Stage**. At this point, adults tend to seek someone else to share their lives with and without such commitment, may fear and experience isolation. Intimacy does not just refer to sexual intimacy but to intimacy between individuals in general. Human beings need friends, romantic partners, spouses, or even parents. A secondary, but similar view, given by **Daniel Levinson**, does not focus on a crisis, but on the **transition** from one role into another and the expectations which accompany each role. Typically, most individuals from ages seventeen to twenty two experience the adult transition of leaving adolescence and beginning to make adult choices. Many individuals desire to then settle down and establish a general timeline for careers and families.

Roger Gould researched changes of early adults. For his subjects, he focused on men and women between the ages of sixteen and sixty. After researching, he found that as adults aged and grew, they attempted to become more tolerant of themselves. Early adulthood is generally viewed as a time of great instability when compared with middle or later adulthood. Gould believed this suggested a correlation between mental disorders and early adulthood.

Some of the significant events and intimacy categories are listed below:

- **Friendship**
    - Establishing friendship relationships is relatively easy during early adulthood.
    - College, work, religious activities, and sports provide ways to meet people and to make friends.
    - Male friendships tend to be based more on shared activities than female friendships.
    - Women tend to make more emotional friendships.
    - Cross-gender friendships help an individual to learn more about the opposite gender.
    - Various levels of friendships continue until and through marriage.

- **Mate Selection**
    - **Theory of Propinquity:** the tendency to marry people who are geographically close.
    - **Theory of Homogamy:** the tendency to marry people of similar demography.
    - **Complimentary Needs Theory:** the tendency to marry someone who has opposite or lacking qualities of a particular individual.
    - **Exchange Theory:** mate selection is a rational economic theory of costs and benefits.

- **Cohabitation**
    - Forty percent of individuals in the USA live together before the marriage
    - Statistically speaking, cohabitation does not strengthen marriage.
        - Cohabitants tend to be more liberal and therefore accepting of the ideal of divorce.

Life Span Developmental Psychology

- - There may be a lower commitment level implied by cohabitation.
- **Marriage**
  - In recent history, the USA is experiencing the highest proportion of unmarried adult than ever before.
  - Marriage appears to be occurring later, but not rejected altogether.
  - The median age for marriage in the USA, for males is 24 and for females is 22.
  - Factors for a successful marriage include: marrying older, sharing similar background/values/interests, and a similar perception of the equality of marriage.
    - **John Gottman**
      - Marital 90% percent of the time.
      - There should be at least five positive comments for every one negative comment made.
      - Conflict can be beneficial when kept within the boundaries of mutual respect.
    - **Hostile/engages and hostile/detached couples**
      - High levels of negative comments
      - Not balanced with humor or affection and can lead to withdrawing
    - **Types of Communication**
      - **Validating:** respectful and listening
      - **Avoidant:** conflict minimization
      - **Volatile:** frequent arguments balanced by humor and affection
- **Parenthood**
  - **Erik Erikson** used the term **generativity** to describe parenthood.
  - Non-biological parent experience similar challenges of child-rearing as biological parents.
  - Blended families are becoming more common.
  - Couples who chosen to not have children are becoming more common.

Life Span Developmental Psychology

- **Types of Love**
  - **Sternberg's Triangular Theory of Love**
    - Passion, intimacy, and commitment are three types of love
      - **Passion:** sexual attraction and 'being in love'
      - **Intimacy:** attachment, closeness, and connectedness
      - **Commitment:** shared achievements and plans
    - Each type of love in a different combination yields a total of seven types of love:

Types of Love	Intimacy	Passion	Commitment
Friendship	X		
Infatuation		X	
Empty Love			X
Romantic Love	X	X	
Companionate Love	X		X
Fatuous Love		X	X
Consummate Love	X	X	X

- **Divorce**
  - The USA has the highest divorce rate of any industrialized country
  - Fifty percent of marriages end in divorce
  - No-fault divorce laws have led to a rise in divorce over the last 50 years.
- **Spousal Abuse**
  - More common in recent years
  - Twelve percent of all spouses push, grab, or shove each other in the USA.
  - Common couple violence
    - Both partners engage in violent outbursts of yelling or physicality
    - Men and women have an equal likelihood of initiating violence
  - Patriarchal terrorism
    - Males dominate the relationship
    - Women are degraded, isolated, or punished
    - Leads to battered woman syndrome

- Victim is often blamed for her own abuse

Vocational Achievement in Early Adulthood:

Work and productivity are important to young adults because they provide fulfillment and a sense of purpose. Being unemployed or losing one's job can cause stress which leads to more instability in early adulthood. In recent years, there have been many changes in the work place. The working population has shifted from manufacturing to service. In addition, the workforce has become much more diversified than in recent years. More races are representing more percentages of the workforce. In developing countries, the majority of the workforce is male, while in the USA, 46% percent of the workforce is female.

Due to such influential changes in the workplace, the implications for young adults have changed. It is impractical to think that an individual is going to remain in their first job for life. Being flexible is the key to moving through the workplace and finding a position in which the individual feels satisfied and fulfilled. People are moving in and out of the workforce every day and for many reasons. Families begin, divorce happens, families move, to name a few. Many families are forced to be dual-income families, making child-rearing more complex than in previous decades. It has become more complicated than before to coordinate family activities and logistics.

Chapter 8: Review Questions

1. The state of physical decline which begins during early adulthood, is:
    a. Disability
    b. Senescence
    c. Impairment
    d. Stagnation

2. The first stage of dialectal thinking is:
    a. Thesis
    b. Antithesis
    c. Creative synthesis
    d. All of the above

3. **Erikson's** terms for guiding the next generation is:
    a. Intimacy
    b. Stagnation
    c. Generativity
    d. Isolation

4. Studies show that early adulthood roles are:
    a. Changing more quickly than in adolescence
    b. More stressful than in adolescence
    c. Easier to perform because of better physical health
    d. A and B

5. Which of the following is not one of **Sternberg's** three main dimensions of love?
    a. Commitment
    b. Passion
    c. Infatuation
    d. Intimacy

6. Which theory, in regards to eating disorders, emphasizes the unrealistic cultural expectations of thinness?
    a. Cultural Image Theory
    b. Regression Theory
    c. Control Theory
    d. None of the above

7. Post-secondary college education (higher education):
    a. Reduces career aspirations
    b. Reduces a feeling of control
    c. Increases tolerance
    d. All of the above

8. Which theory of mate selection indicates the tendency to marry someone of close geographical proximity?
    a. Homogamy
    b. Propinquity
    c. Exchange
    d. Complimentary Needs

9. Studies indicate cohabitation:
    a. Strengthens marriage
    b. Does not strengthen marriage
    c. Increases spousal abuse
    d. Is more popular with women than men

10. **Gottman's** research on marriage emphasizes the importance of:
    a. Not having conflict
    b. Keeping conflict respectful
    c. Maintaining a 5:1 ration of positive comments to negative comments
    d. Both B and C

Life Span Developmental Psychology

Chapter 8 Answers:

1. B
2. A
3. C
4. D
5. C
6. A
7. C
8. B
9. B
10. D

Chapter 9: Middle Adulthood

Overview:
This chapter will provide a brief overview of the physical, cognitive, social, and emotional development of individuals within this developmental group. There tend to not be many concerns and conflicts during these years. Social dynamics outside of the family tend to play less of an influential role than familial social dynamics.

Objectives:
By the end of this chapter, you should be able to recognize, understand, and explain:

- Physical changes during middle adulthood including sexual and reproductive changes
- The impact of lifestyle on the middle age adult
- Compare and contrast fluid intelligence and crystallized intelligence
- The "Big Five" stable personality traits
- Family Dynamics-sandwich generation, marriage, divorce, etc.
- Work-related issues associated with middle adulthood

Physical Development in Middle Adulthood:
By the time an individual passes their 40th birthday, there are visible signs of aging. Signs of aging include, but are not limited to, gray hair, thinning hair, wrinkles, changes in bone density, and changes in body shape. Due to changes in bone density, a person may seem to 'shrink' as the bones lose strength and the intercostal discs of the vertebrae loose elasticity. In the USA, many people become overweight in later life. Each body system undergoes a decline.

- **Hearing**
    - Sex, genes, and age affect hearing
    - Men begin to lose hearing around age 30 and women around age forty-five or fifty.
    - The range of losses varies some loose higher frequencies before lower frequencies.
- **Vision**
    - Visual acuity (ability to focus at a distance) is highly variable with age
    - Vision decline is closer related to genetics than chronological age

- If glasses are required before age twenty, the individual is probably nearsighted
- **Astigmatism** is the lack of elasticity of the lens and is more likely to occur with age
- **Presbyopia** is the technical term for age-related eye changes
- **Glaucoma** is the increased pressure inside of the eye and is more common after age forty
    - Increased pressure squeezes the optic nerve which can lead to blindness, but it can be treated
- **Cataracts** are cloudy lenses which are less serious than other issues. Cataracts can be surgically corrected

- **Body System Changes**
    - Cardiovascular and digestive systems continue to decline
    - Immune system starts to decline and is more likely to attack itself

- **Lifestyle Factors and Nutrition**
    - More than 50% of death and disease are due to lifestyle, not age
    - Heart disease and cancer are the two leading causes of death in the USA
    - Alcohol dependence is most common around age forty
    - Cigarette smoking contributes to death and disease, which usually cause lung cancer
    - Excess dietary fat is a major contributor to heart disease
    - Low fiber intake may increase the risk of colon cancer
    - Over 40% of middle-aged Americans are obese
    - Moderate exercise can decrease health risks and enhance cognition

- **Variations in Health Between Men and Women**
    - Men have a higher mortality rate than women during middle age
    - Men are also twice as likely to die of any cause and three times more likely to die of heart disease
    - Women have higher morbidity (disease) rates than men of the same age range
    - Women have higher disability rates

- Cancer risk is the same between genders (except for reproductive cancers which are higher in women)
- **Reproductive System: Women**
  - Women generally reach menopause between ages 42-58 **Menopause** is the cessation of menstruation and a drop of estrogen
  - The time before menopause is termed **perimenopause**
  - **Climacteric** is the general term to describe a decrease in infertility with age
  - Symptoms of female climacteric are shorter, more irregular periods, hot flashes, and cold sweats
  - **Hormone Replacement Theory (HRT)** replaces lost hormones.
    - May be beneficial for symptoms from lost hormones
    - May increase risk for breast cancer and other illnesses
  - **Reproductive System: Men**
    - No male menopause (biologically speaking)
    - **Male climacteric** involves lower testosterone production, a decline in infertility, and erectile difficulty.
    - Decrease of sperm production

Cognitive Development in Middle Adulthood:

During middle adulthood, information processing is maintained and enhanced by life experiences. In recent years, it was believed that information processing and intelligence peaked at twenty one years of age. It has been discovered that intelligence and processing information continue to increase, as was shown by increasing IQ test scores of thirty-six-year-olds.

There are different types of intelligence:

- **Crystallized Intelligence:** involves accumulated facts and information and lasts through middle adulthood
- **Fluid Intelligence:** involves reasoning, decision making, memory, processing speed, and abstract thinking. This begins to decline around age thirty and is evidenced in slower reaction times and cognition
- **Practical Intelligence:** involves defining behavior, conflict resolution capacity, and problem solving, which is a synthesized form of fluid and crystalized intelligence

There are different **Intelligence Theories**, and each type has its own neurological network in the brain.

- **General Intelligence**
    - Proposed by **Charles Spearman**
    - Basic analytic reasoning
- **Multiple Intelligence**
    - Proposed by **Howard Gardner**
    - Involved in linguistic, logical-mathematical, musical, spatial, body-kinesthetic, inter and intrapersonal, naturalistic, and philosophical intelligences
- **Triarchic Intelligence**
    - Proposed by **Sternberg**
    - Analytic, creative, and practical intelligences
- **Expert versus Novices**
    - **Experts**: are more experienced, intuitive and rely on accumulated knowledge
    - **Novice**: rely more on procedure

Psychosocial Development:

The point of middle adulthood is when society generally recognizes an individual is in their 'midlife' period. **Erik Erikson** proposed that during middle adulthood an individual is in the **Generativity versus Stagnation Phase**. During this phase, the adult is seeking to be productive through work and/or child-rearing. The overriding thought of this phase is the notion of leaving something to the next generation. Without this feeling of generativity, **Erikson** purported that the adult will feel empty and purposeless or stagnated. There are many changes which occur during middle adulthood, such as rebalancing family and work, reexamining marriages, and potentially a 'midlife crisis.' The notion of a 'midlife crisis' is a portion of the theories of both **Levinson** and **Erikson**, which said middle adulthood is a time of rapid change of an individual's roles which may lead to a 'crisis.'

Personality appears to be somewhat stable throughout life. Many personality researchers support the idea that there are five clusters of traits which remain the most stable, the **Big Five**. The Big Five include the stable characteristics of: extroversion, agreeableness, conscientiousness, neuroticism, and openness to new ideas. There are two notable changes to one's personality, during this age: an individual generally becomes more generative and typical gender roles tend to become more pliable to allow each gender to explore the other roles.

Research into personality types has led to the classification of three different types.

- **Type A**: these individuals tend to be more aggressive, perfectionists, and are driven in high-pressure situations. They also experience higher levels of stress, which may contribute to high blood pressure.
- **Type B**: these individuals tend to be less competitive and calmer, than Type A personalities.
- **Type C**: these individuals tend to hold negative emotions and may have a higher risk for developing cancer in later life.

Social Dynamics:

Middle adulthood is an important generation due to serving as the linkage between the generations of early adulthood and later adulthood. Generally speaking, this role of linkage brings both joy and stress. Middle adulthood is often referred to as 'the sandwich generation' due to these individuals caring for aging parents and their own children. The children of these individuals are changing during this age range as well. They are becoming more independent which causes parents to have to reorganize their thinking towards their children. When children leave the house, parents may experience "empty nest" syndrome due the distance between their children and themselves. Priorities must be renegotiated in order to avoid or lessen depression as a result of the significant changes during this age range. Another issue which may arise is if adult children "return to the nest" due to financial or educational constraints. If children return to their parents' house, the parents will have to reorganize their lives again. There are a few significant events which may occur during this age range:

- **Marriage and Intimate Relationships**
    - Adults who are married through middle age tend to be happily married.
    - Twenty percent of women and 3% of men admit to being victims of heterosexual violence.
    - Heterosexual violence is often linked to male dominance, drugs, alcohol, low impulse control, and low self-esteem.
        - Those who experience abuse may feel as if they cannot leave the situation.
    - Divorce during middle adulthood may be more difficult than in earlier years for a variety of reasons.

- **Grand parenting**
    - This role typically begins during middle adulthood.
    - **Bernice Neugarten** postulated there are three forms of grand parenting:
        - **Remote:** distant, but honored and obeyed
        - **Involved:** active in the daily life of the child and may even live with the child
        - **Companionate:** independent and friendly relationship with the child and they tend to live separately
    - The grandparent role is highly variable and ranges from entirely removed to surrogate parenting.
- **Career Considerations**
    - Work is evaluated in many ways, extrinsically and intrinsically. Extrinsic and intrinsic rewards influence one another.
        - **Extrinsically Reward and Motivation:** money and salary; those who rely on extrinsic reward may feel burnout or feel alienated from the work they perform.
        - **Intrinsically Reward and Motivation:** personal satisfaction gained from work; those who rely on intrinsic reward may be happier with their work.
    - Career changes may occur due to physical or mental capability fluctuations.
    - Rapid shifts in technology may move someone out of the job market.

Chapter 9: Review Questions

1. The increased pressure of the fluid of the eye is:
    a. Cataracts
    b. Astigmatism
    c. Glaucoma
    d. Presbyopia

2. During middle adulthood, women:
    a. Have higher mortality rates
    b. Have higher morbidity rates
    c. Have higher disability rates
    d. Both B and C

3. The type of intelligence comprised of accumulated facts is:
    a. Fluid Intelligence
    b. Practical Intelligence
    c. Crystallized Intelligence
    d. Multiple Intelligence

4. Remote grandparents are:
    a. Distant but honored
    b. Active in the daily life of their grandchildren
    c. Independent but still involved in their grandchildren's lives
    d. Ones who live in the same house as their grandchildren

5. During middle adulthood, an individual falls into which of **Erikson's** psychosocial development stages?
    a. Intimacy versus Isolation
    b. Integrity versus Despair
    c. Industry versus Inferiority
    d. Generativity versus Stagnation

6. Practical intelligence:
    a. Focuses on daily problems
    b. Increases throughout life
    c. Defines behavior
    d. All of the above

7. Personality research suggests that there are five consistent personality traits, known as:
    a. The Big Five
    b. Gender roles
    c. Type A
    d. Type B

8. The 'sandwich generation' refers to:
    a. Adults who care for their parents and children simultaneously
    b. Adults who link adults of later adulthood to adults of early adulthood.
    c. Adults who are undergoing significant life changes with their roles and responsibilities.
    d. All of the above.

9. Those with Type B Personality are:
    a. More likely to have an increased risk of high blood pressure
    b. More likely to be men than women
    c. Have a higher risk of cancer
    d. Are associated with calm individuals

10. Common causes of domestic abuse include, but are not limited to:
    a. Male-dominated cultural ideas.
    b. Alcohol
    c. Drug problems
    d. All of the above

Chapter 9 Answers:

1. C
2. D
3. C
4. A
5. D
6. D
7. A
8. D
9. D
10. D

Life Span Developmental Psychology

Chapter 10: Late Adulthood

Overview:
As with previous chapters, this chapter will elaborate on the physical, cognitive, and social development of individuals of late adulthood. In addition, conflicts and concerns which may arise during this age range will be discussed. The key developmental milestones and challenges of this age will be studied.

Objectives:
By the end of this chapter, you should be able to recognize, understand, and explain:
- The stages of physical changes associated with aging
- Information processing components of cognitive development
- Concepts of ageism and the associated common beliefs
- Significance of families and personal relationships of late adulthood

Age Related Demographic Changes:
The media has publicized a 'demographic crisis' of the aging population. The age-related crisis is due to the fact that the 'Baby Boomers' are in the process of leaving the workforce and entering retirement. There are not enough individuals from early adulthood and adolescence who are entering the workforce to compensate for the age differences, hence a crisis.

Ageism:
There are various stereotypes in regards to the elderly. **Ageism** is the term used to define prejudice against the elderly. The effect of ageism is that it prevents the elderly from being able to be fully functional members of society. The negativity is beginning to change due to the field of **gerontology**, the study of the aged. Gerontologists work to provide alternative viewpoints on aging and divide the aging population into two categories based on health: the **Young Old** are more likely to be healthy, financially secure, and happy; the **Old Old** are more likely to have significant mental, physical, and/or social problems.

Physical Changes of Late Adulthood:
- **General Aging**
    - Apparent physical changes occur
    - Changes in tissue and organs
    - Skin, hair, and body shapes change

- o Bones weaken and body weight may be reduced
- o Slowing of behavioral changes
- **Sleep Pattern Changes**
  - o Central Nervous System (CNS) changes, leading to sleep changes
  - o Required hours of sleep remain the same during this period
  - o Amount of REM sleep remains the same as before
  - o As people age, individuals sleep less soundly
- **Changes in the Senses**
  - o All senses decline with age. By around age seventy, the deficits can be found in all senses.
    - Vision
      - Ten percent of the elderly do not need glasses, while an estimated 80% need corrective eyewear
      - The remaining 10% of the population may have one of the previous eye conditions mentioned
      - **Presbyopia** is a common elderly affliction
      - **Senile Macular Degeneration** is the deterioration of the retina and it affects one out of six people after age seventy-four. A diagnosis of diabetes increases the risk of developing macular degeneration
    - Hearing
      - Hearing issues affect one-third of the population
      - Many individuals do not seek immediate help for their hearing problems
      - There is a stigma against using hearing aids due to the notion of them being a symbol of old age
- **Changes in other Systems**
  - o All body systems become less efficient with age
  - o Heart beats more slowly
  - o Lungs lose elasticity of the membrane wall, therefore losing capacity
  - o Sexual responses and desires slow

- Digestion and absorption slow
- Adjustments often have to be made in order to maintain daily functioning

Health Problems of Late Adulthood:

During late adulthood, there is an increase of incidence of chronic disease. The most common chronic diseases are arthritis and hypertension. There is also an increase of acute disease among this age range, with the most common acute illnesses being heart attack and stroke. Women have higher rates of chronic disease during late adulthood, while men have higher rates of heart disease. Regardless of gender, the leading causes of death during this age period are heart disease and cancer. Death from infectious disease rises during this age. The increase of disease is most likely due to immune-senescence, the slowing of the immune response.

Heart disease is not typically a result of the aging process, although cardiac processes lose efficiency due to chronological age. The significant factors to increase the risk of cardiac disease are lack of exercise, smoking, poor diet, and high blood pressure. Cancer is responsible for approximately 25% of deaths among the elderly. There are numerous risk factors for cancer. Cancer begins before there are visible symptoms. Immuno-senescence increases the likelihood of cancer.

There are two areas of significant importance during late adulthood:

- **Nutrition**
    - Vitamin and mineral needs increase with age, while caloric requirements decrease with age
        - Elderly individuals need to ingest more nutrients with less calories
    - Aging cells hold water less efficiently, requiring more water
    - The elderly need to continue to exercise to keep multiple body systems healthy
- **Sexual Activities**
    - There is generally no biological imperative to suddenly end sexual activity
    - While there may be a decline in sexual activity, many individuals still have a healthy sex life into late adulthood
    - Approximately 70% of individuals in late adulthood continue sexual activity

Aging Theories:
1. **Wear and Tear Theory**

This is the oldest and most general aging theory. This theory postulates that the body wears out after being lived in and body parts deteriorate. The body is like a machine which wears out after too much use.

2. **Cellular Accidents**

   Every time a cell divides, there is a chance for mistakes to occur. Generally these mistakes are benign and do not cause problems. The only times these mistakes become a problem are when several mistakes occur together. Mutated cells have a decreased function as opposed to non-mutated cells. There are also free radicals, atoms with unpaired electrons, which may cause harm to the body. Free radicals are produced during metabolism and may damage DNA. Antioxidants such as Vitamin C and E soak up free radicals.

3. **Error Catastrophe**

   Error catastrophe occurs when the body can no longer contain the cell damage caused by cellular accidents. This aging theory helps to explain cancer and malignant tumors.

4. **Immuno-senescence**

   Aging and getting older are part of the life cycle. Researchers believe there is a programmed senescence for each cell. This notion is evidenced by the maximum lifespan. For humans, the maximum lifespan appears to be approximately one hundred and twenty years. Life span is not the same as life expectancy, which is approximately seventy to eighty years. Life span and life expectancy are different for each gender.

5. **Genetic Clock**

   The theory of a genetic clock is congruent with the idea of a programmed senescence. The genetic clock mostly likely resides in the ends of chromosomes, called **telomeres**. The evidence that genes help to regulate aging is shown well in individuals with Down syndrome. Individuals with Trisomy 21 (Down syndrome) typically do not live into late adulthood. These individuals typically die of heart disease or Alzheimer's, which are diseases typical of late adulthood. Another genetic disease, **progeria**, shows the signs of aging. This disease results in accelerated aging with patients dying by age fifteen. **Leonard Hayflick** researched the effects of aging and the aging process. Through his research, Hayflick learned that cells stop multiplying after a certain number of divisions, regardless of cell condition. This number, the cap on divisions, is termed **Hayflick Limit.** The Hayflick Limit is different for each cell.

Cognitive Development:
After the age of sixty, many individuals begin to experiences cognitive decline. Such declines are most noticeable in information processing, which includes a number of categories:

- **Sensory Register:** this category is the first aspect of memory and functions for a split second.
- **Working** or **Short-Term Memory:** this category handles the current mental activity and begins to show noticeable declines in old age.
- **Implicit Memory:** this category of memory functions with the unconscious part of the brain and is responsible for automatic memory.
- **Explicit Memory:** this category is involved with the conscious portion of the brain and is responsible for learned words, facts, and concepts.
- **Control Processes:** this category is also called the executive function and is responsible for the regulation of information flow.

Another issue that elderly individuals often face is **negative self-stereotyping**. Negative self-stereotyping is a self-fulfilling prophecy. The more an elderly person holds a negative view of themselves, the more they become negative.

Dementia and Alzheimer's:
Dementia is extreme memory loss that begins with minor lapses in memory. As dementia progresses, the minor lapses become greater and eventually the individual may forget family members or their own identity. The loss of memory is irreversible due to being caused by organic brain disease. Dementia is not 'normal', even in older age. Subcortical dementia begins in the lower part of the brain, beginning with motor impairments and leading to cognitive impairment. Huntington's and Parkinson's disease are subcortical dementias.

The most common form of dementia is **Alzheimer's disease.** Alzheimer's disease occurs because the neurofibrillary tangles of the brain begin to destroy normal brain function. There are other organic causes of dementia, for example, **Pick's disease**. In Pick's disease, there is an atrophy of the frontal and temporal lobes, and always proves fatal. The cause of Pick's disease is unclear, but genetics are implicated. Another cause of dementia is infectious disease, such as HIV. In the later stages of AIDS, cognitive problems are common. When there are cognitive problems associated with AIDS, it is referred to as **AIDS-Related Dementia**. Chronic alcoholism can also cause a form of dementia called, **Korsakoff's syndrome**, which involves the impairment of short-term memory.

Psychological Problems:
Generally speaking, elderly individuals are less likely to have psychological illnesses. Approximately 10% of the individuals who have been diagnosed with dementia have psychological problems rather than physiological problems. Clinical depression is often misdiagnosed in the elderly as dementia. When treated properly with therapy and medications, depression symptoms can usually regress. If untreated, depression can be fatal. The suicide rate in late adulthood is higher than in any other group.

Psychosocial Development Theories:
According to **Erikson**, an individual of late adulthood is in the **Integrity versus Despair Stage**. During this stage, people may look back on their lives and evaluate their sense of integrity.

- **Self-Theories**
    - Begins with the premise of a choice
    - Ends with self-actualization, according to **Maslow**
    - **Continuity Theory**: a self-theory which focuses on how each person experiences life
- **Activity and Disengagement Theories**
    - The Activity Theory stresses the importance of staying physically active.
    - The Disengagement Theory is controversial and says that the person disengages and withdraws from society as they age.
- **Kahn's Model of Successful Aging**
    - Promotion of physical wellbeing
    - Proper opportunities for social activities
    - Maintenance of cognitive ability

Work and Retirement:
More and more people are retiring from the workforce, largely due to financial incentives. Retirement is a significant transition for many people. This transition is more difficult and stressful if the retirement was forced or sudden. Regardless of the benefits of retirement, there are negative aspects, all of which require the individual to adjust to a new life role.

One of the most difficult parts of retirement is the potential for poverty. Before the twentieth century, one-third of elderly individuals lived below the poverty line. In recent years, programs such as Medicare and Social Security have developed to help and support the post-retirement populations.

Relationships and Intimacy:
- **Marriage**
    - Elderly adults who are in long-standing marriages are generally satisfied with their relationships.
    - Older individuals who are married tend to live longer, happier, and healthier lives.

- **Widowhood**
    - Widowers (males) and widows (females) are more likely to be unhealthy and experience illness.
    - Those who lose a spouse to death are at high risk for dying in the following year.
    - The loss of spouses is extremely stressful.

- **Friendships**
    - Friendships remain important into late adulthood.
    - Friendships are especially important among unmarried or widowed individuals.
    - Siblings often grow closer in late adulthood.

Conflicts and Concerns of Late Adulthood:

Older individuals often experience health issues. In addition, they may experience **elder abuse**: the maltreatment of the elderly which may not be limited to physical abuse. Older individuals may also experience an inability to care for themselves. If individuals experience the inability to care for themselves, they may require a long-term care facility. They may also be in danger of experiencing a drug interaction. Older individuals also have to be concerned with having proper nutrition.

Chapter 10: Review Questions

1. Chronic diseases are:
    a. Generally reversible
    b. Long-standing illnesses
    c. Decrease with age
    d. Disease which occur suddenly

2. The category of information processing which handles current and conscious mental activity is:
    a. Sensory Register
    b. Executive Function
    c. Short-Term Memory
    d. Wisdom

3. The self-reflecting examination of one's life which many older individuals engage in is:
    a. Retirement
    b. Continuity Theory
    c. Despair
    d. Ageism

4. The scientific study of aging is:
    a. Thanatology
    b. Demography
    c. Ageism
    d. Gerontology

5. The physical problems most likely to contribute to functional disability are:
    a. Cancer and heart disease
    b. Arthritis and hypertension
    c. Diabetes and strokes
    d. Alzheimer's and schizophrenia

6. According to the **Hayflick Limit**, the maximum lifespan is limited by:
    a. Telomeres on chromosomes
    b. Secondary aging due to stress
    c. Number of times a cell can reproduce
    d. Ability of cells to metabolize waste products

7. Which stage is an individual in, according to **Erikson,** when in late adulthood?
    a. Generativity versus Stagnation
    b. Mobility versus Disability
    c. Integrity versus Despair
    d. Memory versus Forgetfulness

8. Which of the following is not one of the three parts of **Kahn's** successful aging?
    a. Emotional balance
    b. Physical health
    c. Productive social activity
    d. Cognitive ability

9. The negative views and opinions an older person has of themselves is an example of:
    a. Self-stereotyping
    b. Ageism
    c. Dementia
    d. Life-review

10. What is the typical upper limit of the human life span?
    a. 110 years
    b. 115 years
    c. 120 years
    d. 130 years

Chapter 10 Answers:

1. B
2. C
3. B
4. D
5. B
6. C
7. C
8. A
9. A
10. C

Life Span Developmental Psychology

Chapter 11: Death and Dying

Overview:
This chapter brings us to the end of this manual and to the final stages of the life cycle. During this chapter, the physical, cognitive, social, and emotional dimensions will be studied.

Objectives:
By the end of this chapter, you should be able to recognize, understand, and explain:
- How death is an integral part of an individuals' life cycle.
- The social context and cultural differences of death and dying
- **Elisabeth Kubler-Ross's** five stages of dying
- The Hospice Movement
- Concepts of bereavement and grief
- The Four Stages of Grief

Attitudes toward death:
Death is a part of life. It is witnessed and shared by everyone across every community and culture. Social attitudes toward death have changed in recent years. In past years, death was more commonplace due to a short life expectancy of approximately forty years. In recent years, the average life expectancy is approximately eighty years. Death has become its own industry, despite it not being as commonplace as it once was. In the past, death was accepted as a normal and acceptable part of life, albeit a sad part of life. In present society, death engenders fear and denial. Attitudes toward death across the different stages of the lifespan vary widely.

1. **Childhood**
    a. Generally speaking, children do not understand the finality of death until approximately age seven
    b. Lifespan psychologists encourage parents to tell their children the truth if death occurs in the family
2. **Adolescents**
    a. Tend to not worry about death
    b. See themselves as being immune to death.
    c. Generally believe that death is likely to happen to others but not to them
3. **Adults**
    a. Middle-aged adults tend to have the greatest fear of death

b. Older adults are more comfortable talking about death than younger adults
c. Older individuals tend to view death as a time organizer or a reason to reprioritize.

Thanatology is the study of death. The realization of mortality and death tends to make many individuals more responsive to nature, which results in a greater appreciation of creative pursuits, also referred to as **aesthetic sense**. Many individuals become retrospective and begin to analyze goals, accomplishments, and failures of their lives. There are distinct differences of the perception of death between genders and ages. Women tend to be more fearful of death than men, despite viewing it as something peaceful. Older individuals may be less anxious and stressed about death than younger individuals.

The Hospice Movement:

An estimated seventy percent of people in the USA die in hospitals. There is an increasing number of individuals choosing at home hospice services. The Hospice Movement began in the 1970s as a way to humanize the dying process and to preserve the dignity of those in the dying stage. The term **palliative care** refers to hospice care which focuses on symptom management, rather than prolonging life.

The Dying Process

Terms and Stages:

- **Agonal Stage**: muscle spasms and gasping for death
- **Clinical Death**: heart, lung, and brain function cease, but the person can be revived
- **Brain Death**: an irreversible lack of brain activity
- **Persistent Vegetative State**: physiologically dead, but with brain activity
- **Mortality**: permanent, irreversible death

Elizabeth Kubler-Ross postulated a framework for understanding death. Her stages are the common stages of grief:

- **Denial:** refusing to accept death
- **Anger:** anger in regards to why death occurs
- **Bargaining:** pleading to trade places with the deceased, or if an individual does something, then a higher power will bring back the deceased loved one.
- **Depression:** the intense emotions which accompany emotional and painful events

- **Acceptance:** accepting the events which will occur

Bereavement and Grief:

Bereavement is the state of feeling deprived of another human life due to their death. Grief includes complex physical and emotional responses. Grief and bereavement may include shock, depression, loneliness, fatigue, emptiness, and numbness (both mental and physical). Each person experiences grief differently and each person deals with their personal grief for different lengths of time.

Mourning involves the personal reactions to bereavement, which are influenced by an individual's culture. Mourning occurs in every culture, with some similarities between most cultures.

- Honoring the life and death of the deceased
- A socially approved way to handle grief
- Social support for the mourners
- A way to redefine life and the community without the deceased individual

The most difficult deaths to people to comprehend and overcome are premature deaths (death of a child), sudden deaths (car accidents), or stigmatized death (suicide or hate crimes).

Right to Die and Euthanasia:

In recent years, a new issue has arisen, especially for medical ethics committees--the right to die. Assisted suicides have come controversial among physicians, caregivers, and patients. The lawsuit involving **Dr. Kevorkian** fed the flames of the controversy. Currently, Oregon is the only state in the USA that allows for physician-assisted suicide.

Documents such as advanced directives and living wills help to direct the action a person wishes to occur when they are in a state during which they can no longer advocate for themselves. A DNR, or do-not-resuscitate order, is a limited-advanced directive which instructs medical personnel to allow for what is considered passive euthanasia, but not active euthanasia.

Chapter 11: Review Questions

1. Mr. Stevenson had a heart attack, is no longer breathing, and does not have a pulse. He was resuscitated by a coworker using CPR. What did Mr. Stevenson experience?
    a. Brain Death
    b. Mortality
    c. Clinical Death
    d. Persistent Vegetative State

2. One benefit of palliative care is:
    a. To prolong life.
    b. To reduce pain.
    c. To encourage exercise.
    d. The take care of psychological problems related to dying.

3. During the second stage of dying, what does the individual experience, according to Kubler-Ross?
    a. Anger
    b. Denial
    c. Bargaining
    d. Depression

4. The most common advanced directive used in medical treatment is:
    a. Assisted suicide
    b. A living will
    c. Bereavement
    d. DNR

5. Most American deaths occur in:
    a. Hospitals
    b. Hospice
    c. Home
    d. At work

6. Under what condition can a person be revived?
    a. Vegetative Death
    b. Brain Death

c. Clinical Death

   d. All of the above

7. In which age group do people believe they are invincible?

   a. Childhood

   b. Late Adulthood

   c. Middle Adulthood

   d. Adolescence

8. What state are physician assisted suicides allowed?

   a. New York

   b. California

   c. Oregon

   d. Texas

9. Which of the following is a stigmatized death?

   a. Car accidents

   b. Suicides

   c. Cancer

   d. All of the above

10. Which are the two groups who have the highest ratings of suicide?

    a. Adolescents and young adults

    b. Middle aged adults and the elderly

    c. Young adults and the middle aged

    d. Adolescents and the elderly

Chapter 11 Answers:

1. C
2. B
3. A
4. B
5. A
6. C
7. D
8. C
9. B
10. D

Life Span Developmental Psychology

Practice Exam

1. Which developmental domain is involved with acquiring problem-solving skills and learning new information?

A) Cultural

B) Accommodation

C) Mathematical

D) Cognitive

2. A longitudinal study does which of the following:

A) Studies the same people over time

B) Studies different people over time

C) Studies time intervals

D) Studies where someone is on the globe

3. What is the major difference between the theories of Vygotsky and Piaget?

A) The causal role of maturational factors

B) The causal role of social factors

C) The causal role of environmental factors

D) The types of conflicts that arise during adolescence

4. Who developed the Zone of Proximal Development theory?

A) Skinner

B) Vygotsky

C) Bandura

D) Thorndike

5. Who created the ecological model of human development?

A) Bronfenbrenner

B) Vygotsky

C) Bandura

D) Darwin

6. A scientist wants to know whether failure at a task causes frustration. As a part of the study, one group is told they have failed at a task, whereas others are told they succeeded. Failing or not failing at the task would be:

A) An unconditioned response

B) The dependent variable

C) A within-subjects manipulation

D) The independent variable

7. 'Time-out' is on the principles of which of the following:

A) Operant conditioning

B) Classical conditioning

C) Role modeling

D) Authoritarian parenting

8. Cognitive development begins with which of the following, according to Piaget:

A) Sensorimotor functioning

B) Concrete operations

C) Preoperational stage

D) Post-Formal operations

9. Which of the following is an abnormality that is caused by an extra 21st chromosome?

A) Phenylketonuria (PKU)

B) Klinefelter's syndrome

C) Down syndrome

D) Alzheimer's

10. Which of the following is true about a cross-sectional design?

A) The design only deals with geographical information

B) One half of the total sample size is given a placebo

C) Two groupings of the same age are studied

D) One age sample is compared with one or more samples from another age

11. Which of the following describes an inheritable set of traits?

A) Prototype

B) Genotype

C) Karotype

D) Phenotype

12. Which of the following theories is based on a system of rewards and punishments?

A) Psychoanalytical

B) Cognitive

C) Behavioral

D) Social learning

13. Bob is a healthy, normal male. His sex chromosomes are:

A) XY

B) XX

C) YY

D) XYX

14. A researcher studies cognitive development by collecting data from a specific group of infants starting when they are four months old and continuing at six-month intervals for the next 10 years. This is an example of which developmental research design?

A) Placebo study

B) Experimental

C) Cross-sectional

D) Longitudinal

15. Which of the following describes negative reinforcement?

A) A nephew receiving money for good behavior

B) A niece liking the attention when she gets in trouble

C) A daughter avoiding punishment when she lies about her behavior

D) A son receiving money for bad behavior

16. Which type of conditioning evokes one response using two stimuli?

A) Role modeling

B) Operant

C) Classical

D) Social learning

17. As we age, our level of _____ intelligence increases, while our level of _____ intelligence decreases.

A) Multiple; general

B) Crystallized; fluid

C) Fluid; crystallized

D) Crystallized; general

18. Which is the characteristic common to people with Turner's and Klinefelter's syndromes?

A) Sterility

B) Mental retardation

C) Early onset Alzheimer's

D) Chromosome deficiency

19. Which of the following is caused by high alcohol intake by the mother?

A) ADHD

B) ADD

C) Down syndrome

D) Fetal alcohol syndrome

20. Which of the following is caused by the absence of one chromosome?

A) Turner's syndrome

B) Klinefelter's syndrome

C) Down syndrome

D) Androgyny

21. Reece became pregnant one week ago when her husband's sperm cell fertilized her egg cell. What is the correct term for the fertilized egg cell?

A) Zygote

B) Fetus

C) Embryo

D) Ovum

22. Janis is an architect. According to Howard Gardner's Theory of Multiple Intelligences, which type of intelligence would Janis possess?

A) Kinesthetic

B) Emotional

C) Spatial

D) Mathematical

23. What is the core belief of the Lamaze childbirth method?

A) The mother needs to have her partner with her for support

B) The mother learns breathing to help with labor pains

C) Childbirth at the hospital is recommended

D) Cesarean sections are very dangerous

24. Regina has brown eyes, which are an example of her _____?

A) Dominant genes

B) Genotype

C) Recessive genes

D) Phenotype

25. A couple just had their newborn daughter has stubby fingers and a "webbed" neck. The parents are told that in the future, their child may have difficulty with her spatial and mathematical abilities. These characteristics are typical of which sex chromosome abnormality?

A) Turner's syndrome

B) Fragile X

C) PKU

D) Klinefelter's syndrome

26. How do men and women compare on morbidity and mortality rates?

A) Women have higher morbidity and mortality rates

B) They have the same morbidity rates, but men have higher mortality rates

C) Women have higher morbidity rates and men have higher mortality rates

D) Men have higher morbidity and mortality rates

27. Which sequence of the prenatal developmental stages is correct?

A) Embryo, fetus, zygote

B) Fetus, embryo, zygote

C) Zygote, embryo, fetus

D) Zygote, fetus, embryo

28. What is hospice?

A) Religious treatment

B) Philosophy

C) Nursing home

D) Retirement community

29. Which phrase best describes a teratogen?

A) An environmental factor that causes birth defects

B) A social factor that has lifelong negative effects

C) An abnormality in infants of alcoholic mothers

D) A genetic abnormality passed from one generation to the next

30. The_____ pair of chromosomes determines a person's sex.

A) 1st

B) 46th

C) 12th

D) 23rd

31. At their high school dance, four seniors were discussing their future plans. Which one of them appears to be in moratorium as far as identity is concerned?

A) Julie, who said, "I envy all of you. You're so sure of what you want to do with your life. All I know is I want a career and not just a job. That's why I decided to go to college I hope I'll find something that will interest and inspire me."

B) Lisa, who said, "At first, I thought it was a really bad idea when my uncle suggested I come to work at his law firm. But the more I thought about it, the better I liked it."

B) Angie, who said, "I've wanted to work as a cosmetologist ever since my grandmother bought me a doll that you could put makeup on. Someday, I'm going to have my own cosmetology practice."

C) Tiffany, who said, "I plan on staying at home and being a wife and mother."

32. During the germinal stage of prenatal development, _____.

A) Three of the 5 senses are fully developed

B) The zygote travels down from the fallopian tube and begins the process of cell division

C) Proximodistal mobility begins

D) Sex is already determined

33. Which of the following is an example of the rooting reflex?

A) In response to the sudden sensation of falling, the baby brings its arms in towards the body in a hugging motion

B) When a baby's cheek is touched with a finger, the baby turns its head to face the finger

C) When a finger is placed in a baby's mouth, the baby begins sucking

D) When a finger is placed in the palm of a baby's hand, the baby grasps the finger tightly

34. Why is Fragile X syndrome worse in males than females?

A) Females have two X's and males only have one X

B) Females have two Y's and males only have one X

C) Males do not get this syndrome

D) Females do not get this syndrome

35. James watched his father suffer for a year before dying of cancer. James now wants to be sure that his father retains control over any decisions made concerning how, when, and under what circumstances life-sustaining treatments will be used or withheld in the case of his own final illness. Which of the following does this describe?

A) Power of attorney

B) Living trust

C) Living will

D) DNR

36. The APGAR scale is administered:

A) Ten days before the baby is born

B) During their one-year checkup

C) On the baby's first doctor's visit

D) Right after delivery

37. Ricky is playing with blocks. Robby is also playing with blocks. The two boys are not interacting while playing. This is an example of which type of play?

A) Parallel play

B) Simultaneous play

C) Cooperative play

D) Integrative play

38. Compared with Formal Operational Thought, Post-Formal Thought is characterized by being able to:

A) Focus on several things at once

B) Make a choice based on experience

C) Deal with relative and subjective knowledge

D) Reduce the number of problems that one considers

39. Which of the following toddlers is using a gross motor skill?

A) Mike, who is sitting on the rug and methodically picking up every piece of paper and examining it

B) Sam, who is walking on all fours "like a dog"

C) Joy, who is laughing uncontrollably while reading

D) Steve, who is eating spaghetti with his hands

40. Because he now understands object permanence, John will now be able to:

A) Understand there are equal amounts of water in vases of two different sizes

B) Look for the ball that rolled under the couch

C) Solidify Post-Formal Thoughts

D) Understand that a round object contains the same amount of material when it is flattened into a pancake

41. In performing an autopsy on a patient who had displayed steady mental deterioration before his death, a physician finds some brain cells clumped together in tangles, while others are shrunken. The patient most likely had _____.

A) Alzheimer's disease

B) Parkinson's disease

C) Huntington's disease

D) Age-related senility

42. Three-year old Sally's pediatrician is preparing to give her a shot when Sally bolts out of the examining room and hides behind the magazine rack in the waiting room. If her mother subscribes to the authoritarian style of child-rearing, which of the following would she most likely do?

A) Acknowledge Sally's feelings, help her to understand why the shot is necessary, and take her back into the examining room

B) Yell at her

C) Promise to buy her a new doll if she goes back into the examining room

D) Pick Sally up and carry her screaming into the doctor's examining room

43. What is the strong desire for a child to want to do things for him/herself?

A) Autonomy

B) Self-regulation

C) Aggression

D) Self-control

44. What is the term for when a teenager makes new information part of an existing schema?

A) Accommodation

B) Integrative processing

C) Assimilation

D) Acceleration

45. A child is said to be egocentric during which of Piaget's developmental stages?

A) Concrete operational

B) Preoperational

C) Sensorimotor

D) Formal operational

46. According to Vygotsky, children's private speech is:

A) Babbling

B) Used for self-guidance

C) Antisocial

D) Unnecessary

47. Susan was watching a movie that had some violent scenes in it. She then goes outside and tries to act like the aggressive main character. This is an example of which theory?

A) Ecological theory

B) Psychoanalytic theory

C) Social learning theory

D) Role modeling theory

48. According to Freud, a boy who lusts for his mother and fears castration by his father experiences _____.

A) Electra complex

B) Anal fixation

C) Castration anxiety

D) Oedipal complex

49. Which type of play behavior occurs when children observe in playing and are interested in the other children's play but do not actually participate?

A) Onlooker behavior

B) Parallel play

C) Associative play

D) Solitary play

50. Which of Baumrind's four parenting styles makes demands on the child with little or no nurturance?

A) Authoritative

B) Reluctant

C) Authoritarian

D) Uninvolved

51. According to David Elkind, what is one form of adolescent egocentrism?

A) Inflated ego

B) Popularity in school

C) Use of Concrete Operations

D) Imaginary audience

52. What is the term used to describe someone with a complete blending of male and female?

A) Homosexual

B) Heterosexual

C) Androgynous

D) Bisexual

53. Inadequate amounts of food over long periods of time which cause muscular deterioration is called:

A) Kwashiorkor

B) Malnutrition

C) Vitamin C deficiency

D) Marasmus

54. Which of the following is true about the "Big Five" personality factors?

A) They remain stable during the middle adult years

B) They drop off as adults enter late adulthood

C) They are constantly changing and influx

D) They rarely change, if at all

55. Gender schemas are defined as:

A) Knowledge about the opposite sex

B) Beliefs that are passed down from one generation to the next

C) Standards of behavior and attitudes appropriate for males and females

D) Ideas that are solidified during early childhood

56. Identity diffusion represents a(n):
A) Identity that is based on a false self
B) Failure to achieve a stable identity
C) Identity that is based on a false self
D) Failure to integrate one's identity

57. What is the term Chomsky used to describe a child's innate set of mental structures that aid children in language learning?
A) SL: social learning
B) LAD: language acquisition device
C) CLD: cognitive-language device
D) ZPD: zone of proximal development

58. Which of the following adolescents will report the most negative body image?
A) Sharon, a late maturing girl
B) Dan, an early maturing boy
C) Jan, an androgynous girl
D) Cherie, an early maturing girl

59. The ability to associate information from one sensory modality with information from another is called:
A) Intermodal perception
B) Bimodal perception
C) Accommodation
D) Object permanence

60. The ability to "think about thinking" is called _____.
A) Metathinking
B) Mnemonics
C) Metacognition
D) Memory recall

61. Six-year-old Jerry has just 'resolved' his Oedipal complex by repressing the sexual feeling that he has had for his mother for a couple of years. According to Freud, what will Jerry do next to squash his disappointment?

A) Focus on becoming skillful or competent in some area

B) Find a seven-year-old girlfriend instead

C) Try to be a lawyer like his father

D) Swear off women for good

62. Sharon calls her best friend Morgan in a panic. She has a date for the prom, but has a pimple on her chin. She believes that her date and everyone else will know it. This is an example of the:

A) Egocentric thinking

B) Imaginary audience

C) False-belief syndrome

D) Personal fable

63. A boy in second grade has messy handwriting, does not know the alphabet, and fidgets uncontrollably during class. These findings are characteristic of which childhood problem?

A) Down syndrome

B) ADHD

C) Dysphasia

D) ADD

64. _____ is to curiosity as _____ is to outgoing.

A) Extraversion; extroversion

B) Openness; conscientiousness

C) Openness; extroversion

D) Extroversion; openness

65. Sternberg's Triarchic Theory of Intelligence includes which grouping:

A) Analytical, creative, practical

B) Hope, needs, intelligence

C) Decisive, informative, emotional

D) Hopefulness, intelligence, spatial

Life Span Developmental Psychology

66. Evan likes school, reads a lot, and likes to do experiments. According to Erik Erikson, what stage is Evan currently in?

A) Identity vs. Role confusion

B) Initiative vs. Guilt

C) Autonomy vs. Shame and Doubt

D) Industry vs. Inferiority

67. In a basketball game, fifteen-year-old Elizabeth is concerned that she plays just right because she believes everyone will be scrutinizing her skills. What is the term used to describe this?

A) A personal fable

B) An imaginary audience

C) Perfectionism

D) Metacognition

68. Authoritarian parenting is most likely to result in adolescents experiencing identity:

A) Moratorium

B) Foreclosure

C) Foreclosure

D) Confusion

69. In Piaget's Concrete Operational Stage, a child's thinking becomes:

A) Reversible and flexible

B) Solidified for life

C) Irreversible

D) Focused on the future

70. What is the order of dying stages as proposed by Elisabeth Kubler-Ross?

A) Denial, anger, bargaining, acceptance, depression

B) Anger, bargaining, denial, acceptance, depression

C) Denial, anger, bargaining, depression, acceptance

D) Anger, bargaining, acceptance, depression, denial

71. According to Erik Erikson, what is the most important task during early adulthood?
A) Developing close personal relationships
B) Separating from one's childhood identity
C) Achieving academic success
D) Landing the best job

72. Which one of these teens is displaying the notion of the personal fable?
A) Arthur, who thinks everyone will notice the pimple on his forehead
B) Joe, who wants to be valedictorian, just like his father
C) Josh, who constantly speeds while driving his car down the drag
D) Stu, who thinks he will be President of the United States

73. According to Erikson, a male in middle adulthood who fails to acquire a sense of generativity is likely to develop which of the following issues?
A) Role confusion
B) Stagnation
C) Role strain
D) Neuroticism

74. Corinne, an artist, loves to travel to new places, try new foods, and wear brightly colored clothes. Her personality structure would be best described as:
A) Extroversion
B) Openness
C) Enlightened
D) Conscientiousness

75. Grandparents who live in the same neighborhood as their grandchildren and see them every day are considered _____.
A) Overbearing
B) Authoritative
C) Involved
D) Independent

76. In the workplace, many women and minority workers experience _____, which stops promotion and undermines their power.

A) The glass ceiling

B) Exclusion

C) Racism and sexism

D) Patriarchal terrorism

77. According to Erikson, an individual who fails to achieve ego integrity will experience which of the following?

A) Shame and guilt

B) Feelings of hopelessness and despair

C) Identity confusion

D) Low self-esteem

78. What describes the most advanced process of cognition?

A) Dialectical thought

B) Adult moral reasoning

C) Post-Formal thoughts

D) Neuroplasticity

79. A 65-year-old man runs a 100-yard dash and feels very short of breath. This never happened to him twenty years ago. This reflects which common physiological change that occurs with aging?

A) Shrinking lung capacity

B) Lower testosterone levels

C) Asthma

D) Less cardiovascular efficiency

80. Lulu writes for a local entertainment newspaper and is really good at brain puzzles. She would probably test high in _____.

A) General intelligence

B) Crystallized intelligence

C) Fluid intelligence

D) Spatial intelligence

81. _____ intelligence is the theory that intelligence is one basic trait that underlies all cognitive abilities.

A) Fluid

B) General

C) Crystallized

D) Lifespan

82. "Wear and tear" theories of aging emphasize:

A) The degeneration of cells

B) The limited number of times that cells can divide

C) The decline in the number of reproductive cells

D) The comparison of the human body to a machine that wears out as a result of constant use

83. The climacteric marks the end of _____.

A) Reproductive capability

B) An orgasm

C) Life

D) The ability for a woman to become pregnant

84. An eating disorder marked by a person's obsession with "perfect" thinness is:

A) Binge eating

B) Bulimia nervosa

C) Anorexia nervosa

D) Depression

85. Rhonda is helping to take care of her elderly mother and while also helping her newly divorced daughter. Rhonda more than likely _____.

A) Is in a midlife crisis

B) Is on a very tight budget

C) Represents someone with low SES

D) Represents the 'sandwich generation'

86. During a long terminal illness, family usually experiences which of the following?

A) Depression

B) Anticipatory grief

C) Terminal grief

D) Recovery

87. Which best describes individuals who adopt a disengagement theory about aging?

A) As older adults slow down, they gradually withdraw from society

B) The more active adults are, the longer they will live

C) The more active adults are, the better their lives will be

D) Reduced social interaction leads to decreased satisfaction with life

88. Which of the following is the theoretical proposition that the lifespan of any species is subject to a genetically preprogrammed maximum to the number of times cells can replicate?

A) The Hayflick Limit

B) Free radicals theory

C) Lifespan developmental theory

D) Cellular fission

89. Which of the following best describes Bandura's notion of personality?

A) Symbolic interaction theory

B) Social learning theory

C) Behavioral theory theory

D) Role modeling theory

90. Memories of historical or remote events are referred to as what?

A) Working memory

B) Tertiary memory

C) Long-term memory

D) Short-term memory

91. How would Levinson describe adulthood?

A) A long, stable period

B) A period of constant changes

C) Slow changes that happen frequently

D) Stable periods alternating with transitional periods

92. _____ is one of the most serious stresses a person can undergo.

A) Losing a job

B) Retirement

C) Death of a spouse

D) Remarriage

93. What best describes active euthanasia?

A) Acting on the last will and testament

B) Allowing the patient to die naturally

C) Allowing the dying patient to decide which drugs to use for pain management

D) The intentional administration of a lethal drug dose by medical personnel to the dying patient

94. Why are middle-aged adults described as the sandwich generation?

A) They face the demands of caring for both their children and their elderly parents

B) They are responsible for taking care of their children and grandchildren

C) They have to manage finances for themselves, children, grandchildren, and parents

D) It is now up to them to pass on family traditions to their children and grandchildren

95. The _____ theory of aging states that people age because inside their cells, normal metabolism produces unstable oxygen molecules that ricochet around the cells, damaging DNA and other cellular structures.

A) Senility

B) Cellular clock

C) Free radical

D) Teratogen

96. How a female copes with late adulthood similarly to how she coped with earlier periods of life is an example of the _____ theory.
A) Developmental
B) Continuity
C) Psychosocial
D) Lifespan

97. Widowers are more likely than widows to _____.
A) Remain single
B) Have better financial resources
C) Remarry
D) Become reclusive

98. Which of the following best defines grief?
A) Crying uncontrollably after losing someone
B) Practices that vary between cultures
C) An abnormal reaction to death
D) An emotional response to loss

99. What is NOT a stage of mourning:
A) Anger
B) Recovery
C) Despair
D) Shock

100. A 22-year-old patient is terminally ill. After a long struggle, she realizes that death is inevitable and begins to tell her family about her wishes for her funeral service. This patient is most likely in which of Kubler-Ross's stages of dying?
A) Denial
B) Bargaining
C) Acceptance
D) Depression

101. What is the term used to described children's emerging awareness and control of their intellectual skills and abilities?

A) Intelligence quotient

B) Metacognition

C) Preoperational Thought

D) Trust

102. A mother nags her son to do his chores. Later that week, he ends up doing his chores without her asking because he doesn't want to be nagged. The mother's nagging is an example of:

A) Ratio interval schedule

B) Positive reinforcement

C) Punishment

D) Negative reinforcement

103. Margo is 75 years old. If Erik Erikson's theory of personality is accurate, which of the following would be of most concern to Margo?

A) What should I do with my life?

B) What is the meaning of my life?

C) How can I make more friends?

D) What can I do to increase the time that I have left?

104. Which theory of aging states that all human genes are programmed to produce changes that bring about death?

A) Lifespan developmental theory

B) Wear and tear theory

C) Hayflick theory

D) Psychoanalytic theory

105. _____ is the processing component that has two functions: to store and process information.

A) Working memory

B) Knowledge base

C) Language acquisition device

D) Short-term memory

106. Which of the following describes the theoretical perspective of development being based on intrinsic sources of motivation?

A) Humanism

B) Psychodynamic

C) Ecological

D) Behaviorism

107. Dr. Findlay believes that all behavior is learned. She is not interested in the person's mind; she studies only what is observable and measurable. Dr. Findlay utilizes what approach to psychology?

A) Psychoanalytic

B) Psychodynamic

C) Behavioral

D) Ecological

108. If young Lauren's parents encourage her to ask questions, to use her imagination, and give her freedom to choose some activities, her parents are encouraging what, according to Erikson?

A) Openness

B) Identity

C) Creativity

D) Initiative

109. Cohort effects are concerned with people of different _____.

A) Ethnic backgrounds

B) Age groupings

C) SES backgrounds

D) Geographical regions

110. Thorndike's Law of Effect states that when a behavior is pleasant, it is what?

A) Less likely to be replaced

B) Less likely to cause avoidance

C) More likely to be stable

D) Less likely to cause issues later in life

111. In which stage of prenatal development does implantation happen?

A) Germinal

B) Fetal

C) Embryonic

D) Zygote

112. In order to study the effects of music on memory, a researcher has one group of subjects listen to music while studying a list of words and another group study the same list without music. In this experiment, the number of words each subject can remember would be:

A) The independent variable

B) The fluctuating variable

C) The dependent variable

D) The memory variable

113. _____ studies are those in which the same people are tested at different ages.

A) Chronological

B) Cross-sectional

C) Cross-cultural

D) Longitudinal

114. Ever since he was five years old, Jimmy's father has been telling him that someday he will come to work with him in his real estate office. But when he finished high school, Jimmy informed his father that he wanted to go to art school instead. Jimmy's identity status is:

A) Achieved

B) Diffused

C) Foreclosed

D) Moratorium

115. Matt is aware of his thinking and understands that he uses certain strategies to help him remember. What best describes Matt's cognitive functioning?

A) Memory recall

B) Metacognition

C) Problem-solving

D) Abstract skills

116. Cathy is protesting against the recent enactment of the death penalty in her home state. She feels that it is immoral for the government to decide who should live and who should die. Cathy is functioning at Kohlberg's _____ level of moral development.

A) Pre-conventional

B) Post-formal

C) Post-conventional

D) Philanthropical

117. The Moro reflex is likely to be exhibited by a one-month-old if _____.

A) A finger is placed on his cheek

B) The bottom of his foot is tickled

C) A glass breaks on the floor

D) His arms display a hugging motion

118. Studies on identical twins are influential on gene-environment interactions because:

A) They show more results than fraternal twins

B) Any differences must be attributed to environment since they are genetically identical

C) Gene-gene interactions are studied more often in fraternal twins

D) It allows researchers to understand the difference between monozygotic and dizygotic twins

119. Male menopause:

A) Is a sudden drop in reproductive ability

B) Does not exist

C) Is a decrease in sex drive

D) Exists only in men in late adulthood

120. The decrease in efficiency in body systems from ages 20-40 is called _____.

A) Wear and tear

B) Natural progression

C) Homeostasis

D) Senescence

121. What is the term used to describe when many people become more responsive to nature and have a higher appreciation of expressive and creative pursuits?

A) Aesthetic sense

B) Naturalistic

C) Industry

D) Generativity

122. A 14-year-old girl acts responsibly, makes decisions independently, and accepts the consequences of inappropriate behavior. The daughter's parents probably relied most upon which parenting style?

A) Authoritarian

B) Permissive

C) Authoritative

D) Reluctant

123. Menopause is defined as which of the following?

A) Beginning of a dramatic change in women's reproductive system

B) Ending of a dramatic change in women's reproductive system

C) The middle of a dramatic change in a women's reproductive system

D) Estrogen deficiency

124. What is the most significant change in later adulthood?

A) Caring for children and parents simultaneously

B) Empty nest

C) Retirement

D) Sex drive

125. Tanya is a security guard who likes to stay at home when off work, worries about finances, and has a small group of friends. She most likely fits into which category of personality traits?

A) Neuroticism

B) Openness

C) Conscientiousness

D) Agreeableness

Life Span Developmental Psychology

126. Which of the following statements best describes research findings regarding personality traits through adulthood?

A) Personality traits usually change during a midlife crisis

B) Personality traits are generally stable over the lifespan

C) There is a greater stability of personality traits in childhood than in adulthood

D) There are more personality traits that develop later in life

127. Jenny experiences great satisfaction through nurturing, guiding, and teaching skills to her pre-school students. According to Erik Erikson, Jenny is dealing successfully with which psychological task?

A) Industry vs. Inferiority

B) Identity vs. Confusion

C) Intimacy vs. Isolation

D) Generativity vs. Stagnation

128. Allowing death to occur as a result of disconnecting the life support equipment is referred to as _____.

A) Assisted suicide

B) Natural death

C) Passive euthanasia

D) Last will and testament

129. A young child points and says "Truck!" instead of saying "look over there at the truck!" In this instance, "Truck!" is an example of _____.

A) Motherese

B) Babbling

C) Underextension

D) Holophrase

130. Which of the following best describes the difference between male and female friendships?

A) More camaraderie

B) Greater self-disclosure

C) Shared sporting activities

D) Similar interests

Life Span Developmental Psychology

Practice Exam Answer Key

1. D	2. A	3. B	4. B
5. A	6. B	7. A	8. A
9. C	10. D	11. B	12. C
13. A	14. D	15. C	16. C
17. B	18. A	19. D	20. A
21. A	22. C	23. B	24. D
25. A	26. C	27. C	28. B
29. A	30. D	31. A	32. B
33. B	34. A	35. C	36. D
37. A	38. C	39. B	40. B
41. A	42. D	43. A	44. C
45. B	46. B	47. C	48. D
49. A	50. C	51. B	52. C
53. D	54. A	55. C	56. B
57. B	58. D	59. A	60. C
61. A	62. B	63. B	64. C
65. A	66. D	67. B	68. B
69. A	70. C	71. A	72. D
73. D	74. B	75. C	76. A
77. B	78. A	79. D	80. C
81. B	82. D	83. A	84. C
85. D	86. B	87. A	88. A

Life Span Developmental Psychology

89. B	90. B	91. D	92. C
93. D	94. A	95. C	96. B
97. B	98. D	99. A	100. C
101. B	102. D	103. B	104. C
105. A	106. A	107. C	108. D
109. B	110. B	111. A	112. C
113. D	114. A	115. B	116. C
117. C	118. B	119. B	120. D
121. A	122. C	123. B	124. C
125. A	126. B	127. D	128. C
129. D	130. B		

www.ingramcontent.com/pod-product-compliance
Lightning Source LLC
Chambersburg PA
CBHW082122230426
43671CB00015B/2775